Qatar Katrina Fund

Text by **SCOTT STEEDMAN**

Principal photography by **RUSH JAGOE**

Qatar Katrina Fund

10 Years After the Storm

Qatar Katrina Fund

HIS HIGHNESS SHEIKH HAMAD BIN KHALIFA AL-THANI,
then–Amir of the State of Qatar, visits New Orleans, April 2008

To the people of New Orleans and the Gulf Coast,

In honor of those who returned to rebuild,

From the people of the State of Qatar

HIS HIGHNESS SHEIKH TAMIM BIN HAMAD AL-THANI,
the Amir of Qatar, with President Obama, May 2015

America's Greatest Comeback Story

TEN YEARS ago, on August 29, 2005, Hurricane Katrina devastated New Orleans and the Gulf Coast, becoming the costliest disaster in US history. As that fateful storm shrouded New Orleans in darkness, the world watched in horror as the levees designed to protect us failed, flooding 80 percent of our historic city and displacing hundreds of thousands of residents. As a result of this catastrophic event, over 1,800 lives were lost and a great American city was brought to its knees. In the aftermath of this unprecedented disaster, New Orleans confronted the biggest challenge any American city has ever faced. And while our strength was tested, our resolve to rebuild was never broken.

Among those who extended an open hand was the then–Amir of the State of Qatar, His Highness Sheikh Hamad bin Khalifa Al-Thani, who pledged $100 million on behalf of his nation to assist those impacted. This support came at a critical time in our recovery. By partnering with local organizations, the Qatar Katrina Fund quickly got to work, supporting essential needs like housing, health care, and educational assistance.

Immediately after Hurricane Katrina, many of us knew what it felt like to be homeless. To help those who had lost everything get back home, over $34 million was dedicated to housing. Support for Habitat for Humanity helped build 338 new homes along the Gulf Coast. In New Orleans, financial loans were extended to 120 impacted families to purchase new homes, and 100 homes were restored for low-income victims in the historic Tremé/Lafitte neighborhood. Rental assistance was also provided to low- and moderate-income people. Eleven housing facilities for homeless and special-needs victims were repaired and reopened as well.

Our health-care system was devastated after Hurricane Katrina, putting thousands at risk. Among those in the most danger were children. Through the Qatar Cares Fund at Children's Hospital of New Orleans, more than 19,000 pediatric patient visits were provided for uninsured children. Primary care children's clinics and community health centers were repaired and reopened in low-income neighborhoods. In addition, a mobile medical unit was funded so that health-care services could be delivered to remote neighborhoods.

> "We are forever in the people of Qatar's debt for giving us the critical support we needed to rise above adversity."
>
> **MITCH LANDRIEU**, Mayor of New Orleans

Hurricane Katrina also disrupted students. Through scholarship assistance, more than 2,000 students were able to continue their college education at Louisiana State University, Loyola, Tulane, and Xavier. The $12.5 million Qatar Pharmacy Pavilion, built at Xavier University, provided pharmacy students with a state-of-the-art facility. Because of this investment, Xavier continues to be a national leader in graduating African American pharmacists.

While our work is not yet complete, it is important that we take time 10 years into an unprecedented recovery to reflect on the Qatari people's extraordinary generosity. Their assistance has gone on to magnify New Orleans' lasting resilience by creating jobs, fostering community development, and encouraging lasting enrichment. Today, New Orleans is experiencing a renaissance like no other. We have come a long way; it's safe to say we are America's greatest comeback story. Our future is bright, and I am confident this city's best days are ahead of us. We are forever in the people of Qatar's debt for giving us the critical support we needed to rise above adversity and for providing us with the foundation not just to rebuild the city we were, but to create the New Orleans we always knew we could be.

MITCH LANDRIEU
Mayor of New Orleans

A Gift of Friendship

QATAR AND the United States are not just allies—we are friends. Our relationships run deep. I, for instance, went to school in Portland, Oregon, at Portland State University. Then my first diplomatic posting was to Washington, DC, from 1981 to 1986. After that I worked in Spain, Iran, France; it took me 28 years to come back to Washington, this time as Ambassador of the State of Qatar to the United States.

Over those years the relationship between Qatar and the United States has broadened and deepened. Qatar's Education City is home to branch campuses of six American universities, for instance, and there are now many student exchanges between the two countries. Our country also hosts a US military base, and we have very strong cooperation with Americans in various economic activities: oil and gas, of course, but also in science and technology, real estate, and other areas of mutual interest.

I have just returned from five days on the Gulf Coast, my third visit there since I became ambassador. As soon as I arrived in Washington in early 2014, I felt it was important to visit New Orleans and the areas devastated by Katrina. It was such a joy to meet some of the people touched by the Qatar Katrina Fund and hear their stories about the hard times and how the aid helped them.

Qatar is a small country endowed with great wealth. We feel obligated to share this wealth with others who are in need. This is part of our culture; we believe in helping others. Foreign aid is like a bridge—a cultural bridge that helps to build better relations between nations. We wish to use it to bring hope and happiness to people who are going through very difficult times, as the people of the Gulf Coast were 10 years ago.

That's why my country created the Qatar Katrina Fund, which distributed $100 million to projects in Louisiana, Mississippi, and Alabama. The gifts were distributed fairly equally among housing, health care, and education projects. Urgent funding supported projects that paid the medical expenses for Katrina victims, or provided rental assistance to families who had lost their homes, or delivered medical care to expectant mothers and babies. Other projects awarded thousands of scholarships, or financed the restoration of historic homes in the Tremé neighborhood, or built a new community center for young people.

"Foreign aid is like a bridge—a cultural bridge that helps to build better relations between nations."

MOHAMMED JAHAM AL-KUWARI,
Qatar's Ambassador to the United States

We are very proud of these results and grateful to everyone who joined us in this effort. Traveling the region and seeing the fruits of the Qatar Katrina Fund, I feel awed by the people who have returned and rebuilt. When the then–Amir of the State of Qatar, His Highness Sheikh Hamad bin Khalifa Al-Thani, visited New Orleans in 2008, he told a group of Qatar Scholars at Xavier University, "I admire all of you for your courage and commitment . . . I congratulate you on what you have done. In times like these, we are reminded that we are all neighbors in a fragile world."

Since that day, Qatar has a new Amir, His Highness Sheikh Tamim bin Hamad bin Khalifa Al-Thani. He too has nothing but admiration for all those thousands of people who returned to rebuild, and who are making New Orleans and the Gulf Coast great again. The Amir has followed the progress of the Qatar Katrina Fund with great interest and is very happy to see a few of the stories of hope and renewal compiled in this beautiful and rousing book.

This volume is a testament to what good neighbors can and should do for each other. I hope you enjoy it as a gift of friendship between Qatar and the United States.

HIS EXCELLENCY MOHAMMED JAHAM AL-KUWARI
Ambassador of the State of Qatar to the United States

Prologue **The Storm**

HURRICANE KATRINA was one of the most devastating, deadly, and costly disasters in American history. The Category 5 tropical cyclone slammed into the northern coast of the Gulf of Mexico on Monday, August 29, 2005, creating a huge storm surge that ravaged vast swaths of Mississippi, Louisiana, and Alabama. A few hours later, the levees protecting New Orleans broke and 80 percent of the city was flooded. At least 1,800 people died and more than a million others left their homes, leading to the largest mass migration in American history.

On the other side of the world, His Highness Sheikh Hamad bin Khalifa Al-Thani, the Amir of the State of Qatar, watched the tragedy unfold on television. Two weeks later, his government created the Qatar Katrina Fund, pledging $100 million to the recovery of the devastated areas. In the months that followed, 18 projects received funding.

Ten years after the storm, New Orleans and the Gulf Coast are still recovering. This is the story of Qatar's extraordinary gift and its role in the renewal of a legendary city.

Hurricanes Katrina and Rita

$135 billion

TOTAL ESTIMATED DAMAGE

from Hurricane Katrina according to FEMA. $15 billion total damages from Hurricane Rita (2005 USD).

175

MPH WINDS—both Katrina and Rita were Category 5 tropical cyclones.

53

LEVEE BREACHES in Greater New Orleans from storm surges up to 30 feet, pushing 25 miles inland. Some entire parishes under 12 feet of water.

90,000

SQUARE MILES declared disaster area, nearly the size of Oregon state or United Kingdom.

100,000

PEOPLE in New Orleans had no transportation and remained in city.

1 million

RESIDENTS evacuated from Gulf Coast region for Hurricane Katrina (August 27–28).

3 million

RESIDENTS evacuated from Texas and Louisiana for Hurricane Rita (September 21).

20,000–30,000

PEOPLE congregated at Louisiana Superdome; 19,000 at New Orleans Convention Center.

1,800

DEATHS (estimated); 986 deaths in Louisiana.

60,000

PEOPLE RESCUED; 33,000 by
Coast Guard; 6,000 by FEMA;
2,911 by US Department of Defense.

April 17, 2006

LAST BODY FOUND in New
Orleans; 200 bodies remained
unclaimed or unidentified.

40%

OF DEATHS in Louisiana caused by
drowning; 25% by injury and trauma;
11% by heart conditions. 50% fatali-
ties were people over age 74.

1 million

HOMES DAMAGED; 300,000
homes destroyed or made unlivable.
63% of property losses in Louisiana;
33% in Mississippi.

3 million

PEOPLE in Gulf Coast region without
electricity, some for weeks.

31

DAYS after Hurricane Katrina that
Hurricane Rita hit at Sabine Pass,
Texas. First time in recorded history
that 2 hurricanes reached Category 5
in Gulf of Mexico in same season.

Coastal towns in Mississippi were virtually wiped off the map, and more than three-quarters of New Orleans was flooded

A Tale of Two Destructions

"IT WAS PRETTY sobering," says Larry Gluth, senior VP for the charity Habitat for Humanity, who toured the devastated areas right after the storm. "I had grown up in the Midwest, seen the aftermath of tornadoes. Going along the Gulf shore, it was like seeing that devastation for miles and miles and miles. It was really hard to comprehend."

The destruction wrought by Hurricane Katrina was so monumental that neither statistics nor stories can do it justice. Coastal towns in Mississippi were virtually wiped off the map, and more than three-quarters of New Orleans was submerged. Tornadoes spawned by the storm ravaged towns hundreds of miles inland. Three million people were left without electricity, some for as long as two months.

More than a million Gulf Coast residents left their homes during the weekend evacuation of August 27–28. Almost half made it back within a few days, but about 600,000 households remained displaced a month after Katrina, when Hurricane Rita swept through the region and added to their misery. The total property damage from the two hurricanes was a staggering $150 billion—more than twice the damage from Hurricane Sandy in 2012.

Gluth points out that the destruction on the Gulf Coast was quite different from that in New Orleans. On the coast, a surge of ocean water three stories high scraped the earth clean, pushing wrecked buildings miles inland. "Weeks later, sometimes 5 or 10 miles from the coast, you would come across huge berms of debris. In towns like Biloxi and Gulfport, Mississippi, there was nothing left: just foundations and steps to nowhere." Boats and casino barges were turned into battering rams, and storm water reached 10 or more miles inland. Ninety thousand square miles of the Gulf Coast, including all 82 counties in Mississippi and many others in Louisiana, Alabama, and Kentucky, were declared disaster areas. Vital services were wrecked or suspended, some for many weeks.

"'It's gone'—that became a common phrase," recalls Gary Marchand, CEO of Memorial Hospital of Gulfport, Mississippi. "Things that used to be there just weren't there anymore. So many landmarks were gone, street signs. A good two or three months after the storm you could drive along the [Gulf Coast] beachfront and not know where you were."

New Orleans was another story. The eye of Hurricane Katrina didn't hit the city directly, but a huge storm surge poured into New Orleans' network of canals, and the city's levees, built decades earlier, gave way in dozens of places hours after the brunt of the storm had passed. Under blue skies and cruel heat, fetid water from man-made waterways like the Industrial and 17th Street canals poured into the city, plunging buildings as deep as 20 feet under water.

Several hundred thousand homes were inundated and about a quarter of a million residents of Greater New Orleans—about 20 percent of the population, many desperately poor and unable or unwilling to evacuate—found themselves stranded in a drowned city.

An Eerie Calm

"A GHOST TOWN"—THAT'S how everyone describes New Orleans in the days after Katrina, before its original half a million inhabitants started to come back. It took weeks, sometimes months, for vital services like electricity, drinking water, and sewage to be restored, and there was a curfew and martial law for more than a month.

Eyewitnesses like Gluth recall the eerie calm that descended on the flooded city. "The floodwaters sat there

for weeks on end before receding," he recalls. The lush green vegetation typical of the region began to turn brown. Six weeks later, when Gluth toured the city by helicopter with a local sheriff, there was still "just nothing going on . . . few signs of life; people had evacuated and still hadn't even begun to return yet."

The hundreds of thousands of exiled residents watched the devastation on TV, in shocked disbelief. "After a week of standing water, I started to accept it," says saxophonist Calvin Johnson. "It took three or four days of watching—on CNN, MSNBC, it could be anything, could be Hollywood."

Everyone mentions the uncanny silence. Chad Chambers, an architect, recalls standing on a raised section of Interstate 10 with other rescue workers and gazing at the New Orleans skyline. "You see the entire city, and it's completely quiet," he recalls. "You don't realize how much noise a city generates. There was no traffic, no birds, no insects. The buildings were quiet: no AC, no elevator noise, you just couldn't hear anything. It was the most surreal thing."

Then there was the smell. New Orleans is a humid, semi-tropical city, and it was a brutally hot summer. Lisa Birden recalls returning to her house in Avondale after a month in exile: "We didn't even open our refrigerator. They just told us to put the whole thing on the side of the road for the garbage man . . . The whole neighborhood was stinking all over . . . The smell was terrible."

Many New Orleanians reveled in the small moments that seemed monumental in the city's slow and tortuous recovery. "In those first deep, dark months after Katrina, everything you saw around you was gray," says Jim Pate, executive director of New Orleans Area Habitat for Humanity. "Even all the birds had left. I remember the first time I heard a bird post-Katrina. It was just before dawn, and I was sitting on the porch drinking a cup of coffee I had made on a kerosene stove. When the bird sang, it was two beats before I realized what it was. And then I splashed coffee all over the street, jumping up and down, screaming, 'It's a bird! Listen! It's a bird!'"

NASSER BIN HAMAD M. AL-KHALIFA,
Qatar's ambassador to the United States
when the Qatar Katrina Fund was created >

Barbara Lopez, who would eventually buy and repair a house thanks to a grant from the Qatar Katrina Fund, has a variation on that story. She was out walking when she saw someone drinking a take-out coffee. "I said, 'Oh my God, where did you get that?' There was one little coffee shop that had reopened … Then I heard music a few days later … Coffee and music—I knew life was returning."

A Deeply Moving Display of Caring

LIKE THOUSANDS of others, Pate and Lopez returned to New Orleans as soon as they could and helped others to return and rebuild. Such brave, spontaneous acts of humanity were widespread, as volunteer groups and donors from around the world rushed to help. "Thousands of people survived Katrina," says writer Rebecca Solnit, "because an armada of boat owners from the surrounding communities as far away as Texas went into New Orleans to pull stranded people to safety." Pate describes the flood of volunteers at Habitat for Humanity: "faith communities, college groups, individuals who drove their motorbikes down from Denver, couples, retired or semi-retired people, ad hoc groups of six to eight saying, 'Let's go help.'" Some stayed for months or even years, unpaid, quietly doing their bit. It was a deeply moving display of caring.

The Qatari response was just as extraordinary. On August 29, 2005, the Amir of Qatar, like millions of others around the world, stayed up late into the night watching in stunned amazement as the storm wreaked its havoc. He talked to the country's foreign minister and its ambassador to the United States at the time, Nasser bin Hamad M. Al-Khalifa. Two weeks later, the men announced the creation of a philanthropic fund that would funnel $100 million to those in need in New Orleans and on the Gulf Coast.

The Qatari government decided that the gift should have a distinct identity—the Qatar Katrina Fund—and should aid Katrina victims directly, with minimal bureaucracy. The fund would focus on three clear areas: housing, health care, and education. It would stress projects that would have a lasting effect in their communities, ideally a multiplier effect—for instance, repairing a damaged university building would also provide jobs and training. Transparency and accountability were essential, so the fund worked with reliable local partners and engaged an independent accounting firm to audit all transactions.

Finally, an advisory committee of individuals from diverse backgrounds and political affiliations was selected to help identify the best possible gift recipients. As well as Ambassador Al-Khalifa, the committee members were James A. Baker, former US secretary of state; John J. DeGioia, president of Georgetown University; Lee Raymond, former chairman of ExxonMobil; and Laura D'Andrea Tyson, dean of the London Business School. All graciously provided their services without pay.

Here is the story of the 18 projects in the Qatar Katrina Fund, and a few of the many stories of those who benefited from them.

"Americans shouldn't forget their friends. The people of the Gulf Coast certainly won't forget Qatar."

JAMES A. BAKER, former US Secretary of State, member of Qatar Katrina Fund Advisory Committee

Qatar Katrina Fund

2nd

HIGHEST international donation to Hurricane Katrina relief.

15

BENEFICIARY INSTITUTIONS, most receiving multi-million dollar aid.

18

PROJECTS across Louisiana, Mississippi, Alabama.

$100 million

COMMITTED TO QATAR KATRINA FUND

$38.2 million to education

$34.4 million to housing

$27.4 million to health care

$8.4 million

FUNDED PEDIATRIC CARE for mothers and children affected in Louisiana.

$14.2 million

FUNDED MEDICAL EXPENSES for uninsured victims in Mississippi; 1,333 patients received medical coverage.

4,000

HABITAT FOR HUMANITY HOMES built or repaired; $25.2 million funded by Qatar Katrina Fund.

11

HOMELESS SHELTERS repaired in Louisiana, serving over 800 residents; $2 million funded by Qatar Katrina Fund.

$9.2 million

FUNDED HOUSING restoration, and housing or rental subsidies in Louisiana; $7.6 million in New Orleans alone.

$19.7 million

FUNDED SCHOLARSHIPS at universities in Louisiana for students who suffered losses.

A Place to Come Home To

The Qatar Katrina Fund's Housing Projects

HUNDREDS OF thousands of people lost their homes to Katrina. Many never returned. Others came together to gut and repair thousands of damaged houses or build new ones from scratch. Rebuilding the housing infrastructure of New Orleans and the Gulf Coast is a huge process that is still ongoing, especially in the hardest-hit areas: the poorer neighborhoods of New Orleans and the coastal communities of Mississippi, such as Pass Christian and Gulfport.

Within months of the storm, the Qatar Katrina Fund was funding projects to help people rebuild their damaged homes or construct brand-new ones. A $25.2 million grant allowed Habitat for Humanity to build, rehabilitate, or repair more than 4,000 houses in the hardest-hit areas of Mississippi, Louisiana, Alabama, and Texas. Other projects allowed low-income New Orleanians to repair their historic homes or buy their first houses thanks to grants or interest-free loans. Another remarkable program has reduced the homeless population in New Orleans by 83 percent since 2007.

Habitat for Humanity

"IT'S AN ENTIRELY different city than it was 10 years ago," says Marguerite Oestreicher. She's standing in front of three brightly painted new houses in the Lower Ninth Ward, the New Orleans neighborhood that Katrina hit the hardest. Across the road are several vacant lots and two boarded-up bungalows overgrown with vines sprouting bright yellow flowers. Kids on bikes ride by, dodging the potholes and stray chickens.

"We have been given a chance to build it better, the way it should have been built," Oestreicher continues. "Mistakes were made, sure, but now the city is stronger, with more sense of community. The massive influx of outside expertise, all the help, has broken barriers to friendship and communication . . . I lost my home in Katrina, and I can tell you it's a whole new city now. If the volunteers and donors like Qatar hadn't stepped in, I don't know what we'd have done."

Oestreicher is the chief advancement officer for New Orleans Area Habitat for Humanity (NOAHH), one of more than 1,400 Habitat

"It feels wonderful to own a house, but it's even more wonderful because I helped *build* the house . . . I'm so grateful to the people of Qatar."

PAT HEBARD, Habitat for Humanity homeowner

affiliates in the United States. A global organization working in more than 70 countries, Habitat is dedicated to eliminating poverty housing by creating decent and affordable shelter in partnership with low-income families. Since its founding in 1976, Habitat has helped more than one million families, representing five million people worldwide. In response

to Hurricane Katrina, the nonprofit organization launched Operation Home Delivery to assist hurricane-affected families in the hardest-hit areas of the Gulf Coast. The Qatar Katrina Fund helped kick-start the operation.

"Qatar made a $25 million commitment to Habitat; that's the single largest donation that Habitat International received," explains Jim Pate, executive director of NOAHH. "It came at a very important time, just when we were really building up steam at the Musicians' Village [see below]. It was a tremendous beacon of hope for the New Orleans community. There was no one doing anything at that scope. The people of New Orleans needed that emotional uplift: having happy volunteers here, bringing hope, community, emotional encouragement. That gift brought people to tears all the time!"

A "recovering attorney" from Tennessee, Pate joined Habitat 23 years ago and moved to New Orleans to run that city's affiliate in 1999. His team started building its first house post-Katrina in late October 2005, while the land was still drying out. They had already started gutting and repairing thousands of houses in impoverished areas, in a program called *A Brush With Kindness.*

"Pre-Katrina we had 11 staff," Pate says. "Only four made it back. By 2008 we had 63 staff; it kind of surged. Two to three years ago we were the largest homebuilder in New Orleans parish, or Louisiana for that matter. At our peak we built 123 houses a year."

Habitat uses three strategies to make its houses affordable: interest-free loans, volunteer labor, and sweat equity. To qualify for a Habitat for Humanity house, a person must demonstrate a need, be willing to partner with the organization, and be able to repay a low-cost mortgage. "We provide the financing at zero-percent interest," explains Pate.

The average rent for a three-bedroom apartment in New Orleans is now over $1,000 a month. Habitat partner families, as they're known, can buy a freestanding three-bedroom house, all in, for a monthly payment of $650 to $750. Terms vary, but most are between 25 and 30 years.

As for volunteers, Pate's team—one of 21 Habitat affiliates on the Gulf Coast—has recruited 150,000 in the last 10 years. "That's far more than any other organization, and

they've helped us build 450 houses," he says. Today the team runs an ever-changing roster of 600 to 1,000 volunteers a day, housed at Camp Hope, where they get a bunk bed and basic meals.

By law, Habitat has to use licensed contractors for plumbing and electricity, but volunteers do all the rest. And the partner/homeowner has to put in their sweat equity too: 250 hours of work on other houses, then 100 hours on their own. The first part gets the partner involved in the local community; the second brings it all home.

Margie Perez, a soul singer who moved into her Habitat house in the Upper Ninth Ward in 2008, talks about making

In the years after Katrina, Habitat was the largest homebuilder in Louisiana, thanks to a $25.2 million donation from the Qatar Katrina Fund

friends on the job site. "I'm still in touch with the couple who put in my porch. There were people from all over, a church group from Australia, families were coming. I was able to work with all sorts of people. It was such a great experience."

Habitat Across the Region

LARRY GLUTH WAS an executive at Starbucks in the Seattle area when Katrina struck. One visit to the devastated Gulf region convinced him that everything in his professional career had prepared him for this moment to serve with Habitat for Humanity. "It was a wonderful opportunity," he recalls. "I was blessed to be at a point in my career when I could take a year off with minimal disruption." He did, and never went back; today he is a senior VP with Habitat for Humanity International.

Gluth's role after Katrina was to work with the 21 Habitat affiliates across the region, from Mobile, Alabama, to Beaumont, Texas, and help them build their capacity so they could serve many more families than ever before. "It was an incredible experience. The work was being used for such a great purpose," he recalls. The 21 affiliates had built 53 homes in the year before Katrina. One year later they were starting more than 50 a month, and they had completed 1,000 by late 2007. Funds from the Qatar Katrina Fund covered 338 of those homes: 176 in Louisiana, 124 in Mississippi, and 38 in Alabama.

Gluth was very impressed at how quickly the organization responded to the crisis. Thousands of volunteers and donors came forward, and Habitat affiliates from all over asked how they could help. "It was really wonderful to see that outpouring of support from so many places... from all around the globe, especially the gift from Qatar."

10 Years Later

COMING UP ON the 10-year anniversary of Katrina, Gluth says he's "taken a tremendous amount of pleasure in observing that all 21 affiliates are stronger than they were prior to Katrina. Those families are paying off mortgages, those funds are being recycled into additional homes being built, really in perpetuity. That is the beauty of the Habitat model; those funds then serve additional families. Our production continues."

In New Orleans, Oestreicher says, there are still 30,000 houses that haven't been repaired. "It was 65,000 a few years ago, so we're making tremendous inroads, but it's a huge undertaking," she says. "There are still five empty, blighted houses in my street. You see fixed-up houses with families living in them next to places in ruin and falling down. The scars are still there, the city is still in recovery... We are not going to be out of work for a long, long time."

Oestreicher is encouraged by "the tremendous number of folks who came here to help, fell in love with the city, and stayed. They love the lifestyle—and I don't mean Bourbon Street!" she laughs. "It's historic, European, bohemian. It's America but not America."

Pate argues that the gifts that poured in right after the storm were crucial to the city's recovery. "Whether it's with Habitat, Tulane, Xavier, the medical clinic system—the funding that Qatar gave to New Orleans was so across the board... It was such a strong financial commitment. I have nothing but utter gratitude, tremendous respect and affection. And so do many others; you saw it when the Amir came to town—people turned up to thank him for that support, at every venue."

"Qatar made a $25 million commitment to Habitat . . . The people of New Orleans needed that emotional uplift . . . That gift brought people to tears all the time!"

JIM PATE, Executive Director, New Orleans Area Habitat for Humanity

"Music is a great healer"

"WHAT DO you call a drummer who's broken up with his girlfriend?" asks Jim Pate. "Homeless." It's an old joke, but it sums up the logic behind the Musicians' Village, the biggest project New Orleans Area Habitat for Humanity has ever undertaken. The six-block Village, now complete and home to 80 some local performers and their families, was largely funded by a $4 million gift from the Qatar Katrina Fund.

The Village was the brainchild of two of New Orleans' best-known musicians, Harry Connick Jr. and Branford Marsalis, and goes back to the first days of the storm. Pate had worked with both men before, and by sheer coincidence he had his eye on a piece of undeveloped land in the Upper Ninth Ward. "It was the site of a junior high school that had been demolished, five empty square blocks, a good piece of land. I'd got an appraisal on August 15"—two weeks before the levees broke and flooded that whole neighborhood.

When he saw the devastation on TV, Connick, one of the best-selling artists in American music history, somehow convinced NBC to fly him in from New York as a special correspondent. He ended up at the New Orleans Convention Center with a camera crew, watching thousands of stranded people not being rescued. The experience haunted him and inspired a moving song, "All These People."

> "The experience I had after Katrina, all the people who wanted to help—that will stay with me for the rest of my life."
>
> **MARGIE PEREZ**, Habitat for Humanity homeowner

When Ann Marie Wilkins, manager of both Connick and Marsalis, approached Pate, the stars aligned. "Both Harry and Branford had been getting calls from displaced musicians, so they were well aware of their plight," says Pate. "Many had evacuated and couldn't get back. They needed venues to play in. They talked with Ann Marie and decided to get the musicians back home. So they contacted me—and I happened to know a place."

Habitat bought the land in December 2005 and held a press conference to announce the concept of the Musicians' Village, with Branford Marsalis and his musician father, Ellis. Site preparation began in March 2006, and the first people were moving in by June. Some 70,000 volunteers helped construct 82 homes over the next five years.

The original plan—72 to 80 houses, plus a small community center—evolved as the building progressed. Some older and disabled musicians needed extra support, so 10 duplexes with accessibility features were added. The community center changed the most, morphing into an educational facility that provides after-hours courses for children and adults, a music library, and a 170-seat performance hall with recording capacity. The building opened as the Ellis Marsalis Center for Music in 2011.

Pate laughs when he describes how tricky it was getting the banks to sign off on loans for these wandering musician types, many of whom had little paperwork. "We took gig books, letters from managers and clubs—we even had a person on our staff, Sue, who went out approaching musicians at night clubs. Tough gig!"

Not every place in the Village houses a working musician but, Pate says, "99 percent do, and in many cases there are two or more in the family. It's weighted New Orleans: trad jazz, R&B, funk. There's a cellist from the Louisiana Philharmonic, a great old guitarist who could have been Chuck

Berry, an indie folk musician, a Latin musician. Some of them teach now. There are four or five trumpet players who go over to people's houses to give lessons."

The Village has received worldwide media attention. "We had President Obama when he was a senator," Pate says, "President Bush, President Carter, the crown prince of Norway, the patriarch of the Armenian orthodox church.

"We're part of one of the greatest musical traditions in the world," Pate says proudly. "And now it will stay here, we're keeping it here. It was Harry and Branford's vision, and we're helping them achieve it. We're fortunate to be part of that."

Front Porch People
Freddie Goodrich

"IT'S SO GOOD to be able to plant our plants in the earth," says Freddie Goodrich. He's sitting in the shade of an iron-work gazebo in his lush back garden, surrounded by a dazzling array of exotic plants, including many edibles. A fountain cools the air, and wind chimes tinkle. It's a lovely spot to sit and talk on a hot New Orleans afternoon. "Before, we kept them all in pots because we never knew when the landlord was going to jack the rent."

Now that Goodrich and his partner Tommy own their own house, which they bought and helped build through Habitat for Humanity and the Qatar Katrina Fund, they're in it for the long haul. They're putting down roots, just like their plants.

Goodrich has been in the music business for close to four decades, since he was 13. He has played guitar for countless bands, including a long period touring with the Grateful Dead, and spent a lot of time playing and living in Jamaica. But New Orleans is home.

"I'm more from here than anywhere else. I've always felt very comfortable here. When I first came here I heard WWOZ and thought, wow, this is what radio used to be." He volunteered and soon got a full-time job at the funky local radio station, where he stayed for many years. "That's my obsession, helping fellow musicians."

The weekend Katrina hit, Freddy and Tommy left it late. They were in the French Quarter, looking after a friend's place, and at the last minute they found the keys to his van. On the way out of town, they picked up two friends and bundled them into the back. Waves were crashing over the causeway as they crossed Lake Pontchartrain to safety. "We did 80 miles per hour and didn't hit traffic until Texas," he says with a laugh.

After a "hurrication" in Kansas and half a dozen other Southern states, the couple returned to New Orleans as soon as they could. "You've seen the pictures," Goodrich recalls. "You think you're prepared. But when you drive around a bit..." His voice trails off. "Then it was all about rebuilding."

One Saturday night he walked along Bourbon Street and realized he was the only person around. Finally, another musician came along, banging a drum. "I remember thinking, holy shit, how do we recover from this?"

By some miracle, thanks to a rigged-up satellite link, WWOZ got itself up and running again, so Goodrich could go back to spinning discs. He wasn't sure anyone was listening. Then the phone rang and a voice said, "Hey, man, thanks. I was lying on my couch with my eyes closed listening to you, and everything seemed all right." Goodrich chuckles nervously and chokes back the tears. "Music is a great healer."

Goodrich was part of a group of musicians called the Arabi Wrecking Krewe, named after the New Orleans neighborhood where most of them lived. They helped other musicians gut their houses, but it was dirty work and he had to stop. "I got

about four lung infections, and my doctor ordered me to stay away from devastated houses."

Goodrich's musician friends, including Harry Connick Jr. and, especially, Branford Marsalis, got him on the list for the Musicians' Village. He decided he wanted a house right in the middle, surrounded by his people.

Goodrich has the luxury of choosing where and when he plays these days. He has a full-time job at the Ellis Marsalis Center for Music, the linchpin of the Village. The musicians there give lessons to neighborhood kids, and there's a performance space and a top-notch recording setup. "It's a great space," he says. "To stay true to our mission, everyone in the Village will get a chance to make a recording there.

"We've created an old-fashioned neighborhood," he says with a smile. "I call us front porch people, everyone practicing their music, the neighbors coming over for dinner."

"The thing that moves me is that the people of Qatar believed in New Orleans . . . We really remember that."

CHIP WILSON, Habitat for Humanity homeowner

> ## "The people of Qatar are truly offering a gift of lasting change."
>
> **JONATHAN RECKFORD**, CEO,
> Habitat for Humanity International

The People of Qatar Believed in New Orleans
Chip Wilson

CHIP WILSON SPENT many years making guitars, so he enjoyed helping to build his own house in the Musicians' Village. He never knew who would show up as volunteers. "One day it was a group of teenage girls, plus a couple of aunts and two mothers. People with no construction experience, picking up a hammer for the first time in their lives. We had so much fun and actually accomplished a whole lot. I loved the experience. It's a pretty great thing."

Wilson moved to New Orleans 21 years ago with his wife, now his ex. He lived in at least 10 places in the next decade, leading the hand-to-mouth life of an itinerant guitarist and luthier. "Then came Katrina, and things got interesting," he says. "And I thought everything that could happen to a middle-aged man had already happened."

He was living in the upscale Garden District when the storm hit. Ironically, it was his ex-wife who got him out of town. His apartment wasn't damaged but he lost his car, which was parked in Gentilly. "On Music Street," he says with a laugh. "Another irony."

He spent six months in New England, where he comes from, before deciding to come back. "There were signs of progress," he says. "I scoped out places I could play—it's a pretty big deal. Having a home has made it easier to stay. Before, it was pretty precarious."

When he thinks of all the people who helped build his home, he's amazed at the scope of it. "Qatar gave a ton of money. It's just amazing to me, I can't believe it. We're pretty provincial down here in New Orleans. We never think of Qatar, but they thought of us. Hopefully, the example set here in New Orleans has spread to other situations."

Looking back on Katrina, Wilson says it exposed a lot of the city's faults and weaknesses, like corruption and provincialism. Worst of all, "the number of people who have economic opportunities is so small." On the upside, the storm brought a lot of new blood into the city. "People realized how vibrant it is. I'm grateful for that."

After the photo shoot, Wilson heads inside. A few minutes later, he's back and looking angry. "I've been thinking about it. The thing that moves me is that the people of Qatar believed in New Orleans ... We really remember that."

Born with the Music
Calvin Johnson

CALVIN JOHNSON STARTED young, surrounded by music. His grandmother played gospel piano. His grandfather and father were both jazz musicians, as were three uncles, one of whom gave him his first saxophone, plus lessons, at age 7. He first played the saxophone on stage at 12, at New Orleans' famous Tipitina's nightclub, with another local protégé, Troy "Trombone Shorty" Andrews. And he was 22 when he applied for a house in the Musicians' Village in 2008.

Johnson grew up nearby, just across the Industrial Canal, the one that funneled in all water during Katrina. "New Orleans East, born and raised. You better believe it, brother," he says proudly. It was registration week at the University of New Orleans when Katrina hit. He hadn't gone to a class yet but had moved half his stuff into a dorm room, leaving the rest at home. "Talk about a weird time."

At the last minute, Johnson went to Baton Rouge to stay with a friend, with nothing but an overnight bag. Everything that he left in his parents' house, including his saxophone, was "a hundred percent totaled; they had 12-plus feet of water

AMBASSADOR AL-KUWARI visits the Musicians' Village in May 2015: *below,* the ambassador meets with New Orleans Area Habitat for Humanity staff; *facing page,* he's serenaded by Betty Shirley, jazz singer and Habitat homeowner

there for 3-plus weeks." His dorm room wasn't flooded but looted: "It was in a tall building, and the Coast Guard was dropping people off there. They broke into everything and took what they could. I was a victim of that too."

The enormity of the tragedy took a while to sink in, he says. "After about 10 days, I realized I can't stay where I'm at." He spent the next few months all over the country: Baton Rouge, Atlanta, Chicago, Houston, Portland, Atlanta again. "I really was a nomad. Then I came back and was renting a place on Carrollton for a thousand a month. The rents were so high, it was like Manhattan."

He heard about the Musicians' Village, and a woman at Habitat said he would be ideal. "Me and some other musicians, we talked about it in between sets. Then I went to a church meet-and-greet and decided to apply."

Johnson did his 350 hours of sweat equity: "Talk about brutal! In the hot ass New Orleans summer! I did all my work in the Village. It's a cool way to meet people. It'd be like [mimes being on phone], 'Hey Rhonda, I'm standing in your bathroom now, you better get some clothes on girl!' While you're nailing. It draws you together, the whole neighborhood."

Is he happy in his new house? "You better believe it! I ain't renting no more. When you rent, you're subject to the market. We've had 10 years of rent increases . . . people are getting pushed out by landlords and can't even afford to buy in the neighborhoods they grew up in."

Johnson has toured or recorded with many musical greats, including Harry Connick Jr. and Aaron Neville, and has played at the Lincoln Center and the White House. He's recorded two records and just finished filming a small role in the upcoming Hollywood biopic *Bolden!,* about pioneering New Orleans jazzman Buddy Bolden. He is also the artistic director of the nonprofit Trumpets Not Guns and teaches at the Louis Armstrong Summer Jazz Camp.

The title track of Johnson's latest record is "Jewel's Lullaby," written for his baby daughter. He says he came up with the melody while jigging her up and down in the hallway of the house, humming to help her fall sleep.

Jewel Johnson is starting young too, inspiring, and being soothed by, the music in the Village.

Habitat for Humanity

$25.2 million

FUND NAME: Operation Home Delivery

OBJECTIVE: Provide funding to support long-term recovery of region; provide affordable homes for Katrina victims.

RESULTS: Built hundreds of affordable homes in Mississippi, Louisiana, and Alabama.

1,400

HABITAT FOR HUMANITY affiliates in the US.

4,000

HABITAT HOMES built for Hurricane Katrina recovery.

30,000

U.S. FAMILIES helped by Habitat for Humanity.

338

HABITAT HOMES funded by Qatar Katrina Fund: 176 in Louisiana, 124 in Mississippi, and 38 in Alabama.

1 million

HOMES BUILT WORLDWIDE, serving more than 5 million people.

1976

FOUNDED by Millard and Linda Fuller as "Christian housing ministry," to offer affordable housing for low-income families of all faiths and ethnicities.

1530

Treme Branch

Take a Book

Leave a Book

FREE LIBRARY

Tremé/Lafitte Renewal Project

"HURRICANES ARE equal opportunity destroyers," says Stacy Horn Koch, "but it's not equal when you have to rebuild."

Koch speaks from experience. When Katrina hit, she was running the New Orleans chapter of Covenant House, a shelter for kids aged 16 to 21. Within days she had evacuated the shelter and turned it into a community hub with several health clinics, a Travelers Aid center, a food stamp office, and the NO/AIDS Task Force center. Then she got a phone call from the Qatar Katrina Fund. Soon she was distributing $2.5 million to residents of the Tremé/Lafitte neighborhood to help them repair their homes.

Tremé is right behind Covenant House, next to the city's historic heart, the French Quarter. It has a vibrant, 300-year-old culture and includes Congo Square, where both jazz and brass band music evolved more than a century ago. Tremé is still a hotbed of both musical traditions, notably

> ## "When the Amir came down here to see for himself what was going on and meet people, that was an act of extraordinary kindness."
>
> **STACY HORN KOCH**, overseer of Tremé/Lafitte Renewal Project

during the neighborhood's regular second line parades and jazz funerals, which may feature local stars like Kermit Ruffins or Trombone Shorty.

The US Army Corps of Engineers counted 3,429 homes in Tremé right after Hurricane Katrina—and estimated that more than half of them had been severely damaged. The residents who did return (and many didn't) struggled to rebuild their lives.

"A tremendous amount of people wanted to come back right away, but what were they going to come back to?" asks Koch. "These are people working for minimum wage, coming back to homes that are destroyed. They haven't been paid for a month or more. How are they going to rebuild? Most of them just wanted to go home. I did too, but I had resources. For them it was impossibly hard."

The Tremé/Lafitte Renewal Project helped by providing 100 low-income homeowners with grants to cover the cost of repairs, for an average amount of $24,000. "In the end, we made a significant difference in several hundred people's

lives," says Koch. "Once you start working in a neighborhood, they let their neighbors know that there's help coming back."

Koch was impressed by the way the fund managers watched how their money was being spent and made sure it was helping people. There were various stipulations, such as a requirement that the owner stay in the house for at least five years to protect against property speculation, and compulsory (and free) home ownership training and counseling. Koch says the grant recipients were all incredibly grateful for the unexpected gift.

"This is my community, and they supported us. To make it healthy, we needed people to come home. To this day, I think what they [the Qataris] did was extraordinary. When the Amir came down here to see for himself what was going on and meet people, that was an act of extraordinary kindness," she continues, choking back tears. "It makes me cry because it touches my heart. Sometimes it's heartbreaking because of the sadness, and sometimes because I'm witnessing the very best, the goodness in people."

Koch is still amazed by how Katrina brought out the best in people, and the worst. Living for many months in Baton Rouge while her house was being repaired, she met people who were angry at the refugees, and others who opened their homes to folks they'd never met before. She had a friend who was rescued from a canal near Esplanade Avenue by a local drug dealer. "Then you had people saying it was God's judgment on the city," she says with a laugh, "because we have prostitutes and are immoral! And then you had people flying in to help, people like the Qataris with no connection, helping because it was the right thing to do.

"I wish more people were like the Amir in leadership, that there were more acts of goodness. Then maybe we wouldn't have so much horrible stuff going on, less worry about what people believe, and more emphasis on just being good."

ETTA MAY WILLIAMS in front of her historic house in the Tremé neighborhood of New Orleans, renovated thanks to a grant from the Qatar Katrina Fund

"I will be here until the good Lord moves me"

HURRICANE KATRINA'S floodwaters lapped at her doorstep, and its winds howled through her hallways. But Etta May Williams was determined to stay in her Tremé/Lafitte home. She had lived in this famous New Orleans neighborhood for nearly 30 years, and she wasn't planning on leaving. She'd been through many hurricanes in her life, but says "Katrina was the worst."

After the storm hit, Etta May waited alone in her house for five days, her only company a kerosene lamp. When the National Guard ordered her to leave, she was evacuated to the New Orleans Convention Center, and later to Baton Rouge, 80 miles away, where she stayed for four months.

When she finally returned to New Orleans, Etta May was shocked. Tremé looked like a war zone. Water had leaked through the rain-soaked walls of her historic house; most of the plumbing needed repair. A grant from the Qatar Katrina Fund allowed her to restore the place and move back home.

Many Tremé/Lafitte residents never did return, but many more were determined to clean up and start again. In all, 100 received grants from the Qatar Katrina Fund.

Now Etta May sits on her freshly painted porch and watches this colorful neighborhood being rebuilt. "I will be here until the good Lord moves me," she says with a smile.

Tremé/Lafitte Renewal Project

$2.5 million

FUND NAME: Restoration of Homes

OBJECTIVE: Restore homes for low-income residents in historic Tremé/Lafitte neighborhood so long-time residents and community leaders could return.

RESULTS: Repaired 100 homes, helping increase neighborhood recovery rate for owner-occupied housing to 88% by 2010.

8,850

RESIDENTS pre-Katrina in 2000.

3,429

OCCUPIED housing units in Tremé/Lafitte before Katrina; US Army Corps of Engineers estimated that 52% received "severe damage" as result of hurricane.

4,283

RESIDENTS in 2014.

1790

DEVELOPER CLAUDE TREMÉ bought and subdivided Morand Plantation to house Caucasians, Haitian Creoles, and free people of color.

1970

FIRST New Orleans Jazz & Heritage Festival held in Congo Square, Tremé, considered the birthplace of jazz.

12.5%

INCREASE in owner-occupied residences because of Katrina reconstruction.

Neighborhood Housing Services

LISA BIRDEN remembers first seeing her house like it was yesterday. It was an autumn evening in 2007 and Birden, a single mother, had been looking for a place she liked and could afford for months. She was working as a dialysis technician and would go house hunting after dinner. Two years after Katrina, prices were climbing, though not nearly as fast as rents. It was almost dark when she saw it, at the end of a row of houses in Waggaman, just over the bridge from New Orleans. The price was right and the owner wanted a quick sale. Birden knew this was her home, the first one she had ever owned.

Hurricane Katrina was relatively easy on Birden. She was living at her mother's house in Avondale, just west of Waggaman. They evacuated and came back a few weeks later to find "the house was okay. We had some water damage, but it was minor, not like some people. I have a sister who lived in the Seventh Ward. She lost everything."

But the storm made Birden want to buy her own place. Like many other first-time buyers, she would never have been able to put together the financing without Neighborhood Housing Services (NHS) of New Orleans and the Qatar Katrina Fund's housing assistance program. NHS, a nonprofit corporation that has worked to revitalize the city's neighborhoods for 35 years, has for the past decade focused on encouraging low- and moderate-income Katrina victims to return and reinvest in the New Orleans area. Through the Qatar-funded program, NHS has provided up to $25,000 to help 120 Katrina victims buy an affordable house.

"It's a blessing," says Birden. "I've made some money, but I didn't have enough credit, didn't have credit cards or anything. It [the interest-free loan] gives you the down payment; that's the hard bit." First-time buyers like Birden also receive free financial counseling and education.

Sixty percent of New Orleans residents rent, almost double the national average, and more than half are paying unaffordable amounts, up 13 percent since Katrina. One way out of this trap is home ownership. Programs like the one run by NHS give solvent would-be buyers the two things they generally lack: financial literacy and a down payment.

All loan recipients are asked to write a testimonial telling their story; several are excerpted in the following pages. "Without exception, they are stories of triumph over tragedy," says Lauren Anderson, NHS's CEO after Katrina. "The happy endings are all the result of the generosity of the good people of Qatar.

"It is gratifying for me to read the stories of these families," Anderson continues. "The program has been transformative. It has changed lives and given families new hope for the future. We are so very honored that you [the Qatar Katrina Fund] placed your trust in us to be one of the vehicles of your generosity in our community . . . Thank you for your incredible support of the rebuilding efforts of the Gulf Coast."

"I never thought I'd get this far"

ARTHUR AND LOIS Anderson have no shortage of family—she has two brothers and four sisters, and he has five brothers and twelve sisters. Between them, the couple also share five grown children and seven grandchildren. "The way it is in my family," Arthur explains, "whenever one of us is traveling, especially in the South, we don't have to go very far to find the comfort of family."

The Andersons never gave much thought to owning their own home. Two things changed all that. First they got married, in 2004, and began to think about finding a place with more room than the apartment they were renting in Mid-City. Then a year later, Hurricane Katrina hit.

With their apartment flooded out, the couple had to flee the city. Arthur was back within a few weeks, sleeping at first on a blow-up mattress on the floor at his workplace, then at a hotel. He couldn't rescue anything from their apartment. The building was so badly damaged that it was eventually torn down.

When the couple were finally reunited and ready to move into a new apartment, they got a rude shock. "Oh, man, prices went through the roof," Arthur recalls. "We was paying $500 for a two-bedroom before Katrina. After, we were paying $650 for a one-bedroom. It was crazy. People got to live somewhere, man!"

> "I never really thought I'd get this far...
> But my wife kept encouraging me, telling
> me I have to keep the faith."

ARTHUR ANDERSON, NHS/Qatar grant recipient

With help from the NHS's Qatar program, the Andersons eventually found a house that suited their budget and their needs, a spacious shotgun-style bungalow in the historic Tremé neighborhood, just up the street from Louis Armstrong Park. Not long after they moved in, the couple hosted a house-blessing ceremony, with a pot of gumbo simmering in the kitchen and guests spilling out into the front yard.

Now that they have a place to hold family get-togethers and host visiting family members, Lois is extremely thankful. "I thank God every day," she says, "for all the people he allowed to come into our lives who helped us."

For his part, Arthur Anderson is glad they persisted through the long qualifying and purchase process. "I never really thought I'd get this far," he says. "My patience was really getting short. But my wife kept encouraging me, telling me I have to keep the faith."

There's No Place Like New Orleans
Barbara Lopez

"I WOULDN'T HAVE my home if it wasn't for the grant," says Barbara Lopez. She is sitting in the living room of her beautifully renovated old house in New Orleans' Pigeon Town neighborhood, remembering the first time she saw the building. It had been derelict for 25 years or so, but Lopez could see the renovated version in her mind's eye, with French doors, light walls, even a backyard garden with herb boxes and lush bamboo. The problem was getting the mortgage.

"I have always worked for nonprofits," Lopez explains, "and had never had much money. Like a lot of people, I never really thought I could own my own home. I knew I could pay the mortgage, but couldn't gather the down payment together."

A grant from the Qatar Katrina Fund, through the nonprofit Neighborhood Housing Services, allowed her to buy the house and do the basic renovations: "electricity, that kind of thing. I didn't paint the outside until this year, that was an extra."

Though born in Honduras, Lopez has lived in New Orleans since she was 11 years old. "This is my home. I've spent three-quarters of my life here," she says. Like so many residents of the city, she had to evacuate during Katrina. She went to Memphis, then Atlanta, then Charlotte, North Carolina. But all she wanted was to get home.

"Everyone just wanted to come home," she recalls, fighting back the tears that still come nearly 10 years later. Many didn't make it home, but Lopez did. She was back just six weeks after the storm, house-sitting for friends in the Tremé neighborhood. Her apartment was still under water, her car had been washed away, and her temporary digs had a hole in the roof, but at least she was home in New Orleans.

A few days after she got back, Lopez was out walking when she saw someone drinking a take-out coffee. "I said, 'Oh my God, where did you get that?' There was one little coffee shop that had reopened, with a hand-written sign saying 'Coffee, beer, cigarettes.' Then I heard music a few days later, from a restaurant called Angeli, and I knew the musicians were back. Coffee and music—I knew life was returning. Coffee, music, bars—this is New Orleans, after all!"

Undeterred by the devastation still evident throughout the city, Lopez heard about the Qatar grant program and soon found the perfect house, in a neighborhood she liked, with several close friends nearby. "I'm not a hesitant person," she says. "This was my first opportunity to own my own home, and I jumped at it."

Now that the renovations are finished, the walls are hung with art, and herbs from the garden are drying in the kitchen, Lopez has decided to construct a small altar—a common New

Orleans folk custom—to honor the assistance given her by the people of Qatar. Her daughter will admire it when she visits from Austin, Texas, with Lopez's first grandchild, a boy born in March 2014.

"I really love this neighborhood, and love living in New Orleans. There's no place like it anywhere in the world," Lopez says. "Now I'm not subject to the whims of someone else owning the home I live in. I have a place where I can really extend my roots."

Never Been Happier
Shawanda Leggins

BY THE TIME Shawanda Leggins closed on her house in 2008, the 30-year-old mother of three had been through more traumatic events than most of us face in a lifetime. Raised in a public housing development in New Orleans, she had enlisted in the army after high school. Six months before Katrina she learned she was being sent to Iraq, so she

> "I really love this neighborhood, and love living in New Orleans. There's no place like it anywhere in the world."
>
> **BARBARA LOPEZ**, NHS/Qatar grant recipient

left her three children in the care of her ex-husband. She was training in Oklahoma when the hurricane struck, and she watched the disaster unfold on TV for eight days, with no news of her children. She eventually located them in Houston and made sure they were safe in New Orleans before leaving for Iraq.

Leggins was posted to Baghdad's Green Zone, where she was bombarded by mortar fire every night. Six months later she had a breakdown and was hospitalized, then sent home. After nine months, she had another breakdown and her children were removed from her custody. She vowed to get her life back, beginning with saving money to buy a house. She had counseling, regained custody of her children, and obtained both a Veterans Affairs–approved mortgage and a Qatar program loan through NHS.

Today Leggins sits happily in the living room of her four-bedroom split-level ranch house in a quiet area of Algiers, New Orleans. "I knew the minute I saw this house that … it would be a great thing for me and the kids," she says. She's still dealing with post-traumatic stress, but she owns her own home and feels in control of her destiny. "I've never been happier with my life than I am right now," she says.

We Were Meant to Come Home
Frank Myers and Lasonja Washington

RIGHT AFTER HURRICANE Katrina, Frank Myers and Lasonja Washington knew they wanted to buy a house, but they couldn't agree on what kind. For two years they'd been living with their two children in a subsidized apartment complex in Metairie, Jefferson Parish, a suburb of New Orleans. Katrina destroyed most of the complex, but their unit was largely undamaged. "I took that as a sign

that we were meant to come home," says Washington. But when the management company raised their rent by nearly 50 percent, Washington knew it was time to find another housing solution. "Okay, I said, we have to buy a home."

The couple, who had been married for five years, signed up for credit counseling and home ownership training at NHS, and soon qualified for a loan through the Qatar program. But finding a house to buy was another matter entirely. A truck driver for a demolition and waste management company, Myers had some friends and family in the construction trades who could help them renovate, so they could buy an affordable place in need of repair and increase their equity significantly. But the couple searched for close to a year without finding the right property.

In the meantime, Washington, a stay-at-home mom suffering from the autoimmune disease lupus, had become pregnant. The couple halted their home search for several months until Washington had her baby girl. "After I gave birth," she says, "I got a whole lot more serious about finding a place for us to buy. I just said to myself, okay, I want a home for my baby."

They found a 2,400-square-foot brick ranch house in a quiet suburban neighborhood in New Orleans East. "We spend all our free time watching home and garden improvement shows on cable," Washington says.

The neighborhood is inhabited mainly by residents who lived there before Hurricane Katrina, and there's a bus to take their children to a magnet school and a college prep school in the Uptown area of New Orleans. "Without the loan from the Qatar grant program," Washington says, "we never would have been able to find a home as large as this, or one in as nice a neighborhood. We had a baby and found a home all in the same year. It's truly been a wonderful year for our family."

Neighborhood Housing Services

1976

FOUNDED to increase home ownership in urban neighborhoods through affordable housing, education, and community.

378,715

POPULATION of New Orleans (2013).

148,398

HOUSEHOLDS (2013).

189,896

TOTAL HOUSING UNITS in New Orleans.

$3.1 million

FUND NAME: Home Ownership Assistance Program

OBJECTIVE: Provide subsidies to low- and moderate-income Katrina victims to buy affordable housing in New Orleans.

RESULTS: Provided loans, financial counseling, and courses to 120 first-time homebuyers.

150

VACANT AND DAMAGED properties in one neighborhood (Freret) post-Katrina; 264 NHS letters sent to locate absent owners: 70% owners returned after restoration.

27.3%

NEW ORLEANS RESIDENTS live below federal poverty level.

UNITY of Greater New Orleans

MARTHA KEGEL, executive director of UNITY of Greater New Orleans, is beaming. She has just heard that First Lady Michelle Obama will be in town and has asked to meet with Kegel and others from the nonprofit, which provides housing and support services to prevent homelessness. The reason? New Orleans has just been declared the first US city to end veteran homelessness.

In June 2014, Obama challenged 570 cities across the United States to commit to housing every veteran living on their streets by the end of 2015. New Orleans was the first city to achieve this goal, housing 227 veterans by the end of 2014. Since 2007, the city has reduced its homeless population by 83 percent, from over 11,000 to less than 2,000.

These are heady achievements for a city with sky-high poverty and unemployment rates and that lost hundreds of thousands of homes

New Orleans has just been declared the first US city to end veteran homelessness—and they were able to do it thanks in large part to the gift from Qatar

because of Katrina. "Driving these numbers down, it's exciting," says Kegel. "We were able to do that thanks to the Qatar gift."

She's referring to the $2 million grant UNITY received from the Qatar Katrina Fund in the fall of 2006. UNITY is a collaborative that includes 63 different agencies; the grant from Qatar helped 10 of them pay for repairs to their housing units. The organization's motto—Bringing New Orleans Home—could apply to the whole rebuilding effort after Katrina, but it's especially poignant for the city's homeless population, which suffered horribly during the hurricane and the extreme housing shortage that followed.

Kegel estimates that about 2,000 people were living on the streets of New Orleans when the city was flooded. The city had no plan in place for evacuating people who had no access to private transportation, an estimated quarter of the city's population. "I am sure many homeless people drowned," Kegel says. Ten years later the death toll is still unclear. "There is a tendency to minimize what happened, as there was after the San Francisco earthquake. This is a tourist town, remember."

UNITY insisted that all its agencies transport their clients to safety personally, and started putting its systems back together within two days of the storm. The Qatar grant gave UNITY a real shot in the arm. "It created hundreds of units for people to live in, got them back online quickly," says Kegel. "It allowed the whole network, a continuum of care, to be operational 18 months after the disaster, which is just amazing. Nobody else recovered that fast. It wouldn't have been possible without the Qatar money."

Reverend Willie Gable Jr. says that he too was extremely surprised, and extremely grateful, for the gift from Qatar. Pastor at the Progressive Baptist Church in downtown

New Orleans, and chair of the Housing and Economic Development Commission of the National Baptist Convention, Gable also runs the Dr. Murphy W. McCaleb Education Fund, a UNITY agency that funds the housing of chronically homeless people and that received a chunk of the Qatar grant.

Every edifice in Gable's life was battered by Hurricane Katrina. The church where he preaches was badly damaged and his congregation dispersed; his home, near Bayou St. John in Mid-City, was flooded by six feet of water (for the next two years, he commuted 80 miles to and from Baton Rouge); and the two buildings the McCaleb Fund was operating at the time, as well as a third building that houses vulnerable seniors, were all inundated. "Individuals had to be evacuated. They were soon spread all over the place," he recalls. The fund had insurance and eventually got some federal money, but the situation was dire.

"What the Qatar funds did, they allowed us get started with one 10-unit building for homeless individuals with substance or alcohol abuse issues," Gable explains. "These are the chronic homeless. If they didn't have this place to stay, they'd be on the streets." Renovating that facility then allowed the fund to construct a brand-new building with 43 units. "About half are for the chronic homeless, half for low- and moderate-income people, many with disabilities," Gable explains. "We provide case assistance. The majority have some sort of disability—mental, physical, alcoholism, substance abuse."

The McCaleb Fund, which has been helping the New Orleans homeless population since 1990, now operates 78 units. "We are a faith-based organization," Gable says, "but we help all races, all faiths, all genders, all sexual persuasions." When it's suggested that this is fine work they are doing, he replies, "Yes, we're grateful to the Lord for that."

Gable is also grateful to the people of Qatar for their unexpected largesse. "Not only to us," he adds, "but to the city of New Orleans, all the other organizations and nonprofits here. Xavier University, for instance, would not have rebounded as fast at all without that gift—if not for the love that was shown."

Kegel agrees that in the years after the hurricane, the Qatar Katrina Fund was critical to UNITY's efforts to include the poorest and most vulnerable New Orleanians in the rebuilding of the city, by ensuring they had safe and decent places to live. "The temporary shelter and permanent apartments that were rebuilt as a result of the grant," she says, "remain vital today to ongoing work to rehouse people who are pitched into homelessness as a result of poverty, disability, and unaffordable housing."

"I was extremely grateful for the gift that Qatar provided, not only to us but to the city of New Orleans ... for the love that was shown."

REVEREND WILLIE GABLE JR., UNITY partner

UNITY of Greater New Orleans

1992

FOUNDED as collaborative non-profit, leading 63 agencies that provide housing and services to homeless people.

30

UNITY BUILDINGS damaged by Katrina.

2,051

HOMELESS PEOPLE in New Orleans in 2005; 11,619 in 2007; 9,200 in 2011; 1,981 in 2014.

50

YEARS: Average life expectancy of a homeless person; 30 years less than US average.

$2 million

FUND NAME: Repair of Residential Facilities for the Homeless

OBJECTIVE: Repair housing units for homeless and disabled victims of Katrina.

RESULTS: Repaired 11 housing facilities, serving over 800 homeless and disabled residents.

2,000

PEOPLE slept in homeless camps at City Hall or under Claiborne Avenue overpass 2007–2008; UNITY rehoused 20% in those years.

The National Housing Partnership Foundation

"THE MONEY allowed us to provide up to two-thirds rental assistance to anyone who had been impacted by the storm," explains Thomas Vaccaro, a senior VP with the National Housing Partnership Foundation (NHPF). "Anyone who could document that they had been displaced by Katrina, and were low to moderate income, was eligible."

NHPF is a countrywide nonprofit that provides quality, affordable housing for families in financial need by rehabilitating properties and offering training and support for local residents. Hurricane Katrina severely damaged four of NHPF's large housing complexes in New Orleans. Several thousand tenants had to evacuate the city, then found themselves dispersed across the country, not knowing when their homes would be habitable again.

81

The foundation immediately committed to renovating the hundreds of damaged rental units to help fill the lack of affordable housing. Thanks to a gift from the Qatar Katrina Fund, NHPF provided monthly rental subsidies to 131 families in hurricane-damaged communities. The subsidies eased the financial burden on tenants and allowed additional occupants, who had not previously qualified, to live in NHPF's reasonably priced rental properties.

"I am extremely grateful to Qatar and the assistance we received from them," says Vaccaro. "Anyone who stepped up with financial help at that time was wonderful."

In April 2008, His Highness Sheikh Hamad bin Khalifa Al-Thani, then the Amir of Qatar, visited one of NHPF's properties: Tanglewood Apartments, a 384-unit complex in Westwego, a low-income suburb south of the river in New Orleans. "The kids came out," recalls Vaccaro. "We have a program called Virtual Vacation, and they had studied Qatar, learned about the food and so on. The kids presented the Amir with a painting they did. It was real sweet.

"It was them saying thank you to him for what he'd done."

The NHP Foundation

1989

INCORPORATED as nonprofit.

20,000

RESIDENTS served by NHPF; 31 communities; 12 states.

18,000

TOTAL NHPF UNITS: 6,000 housing units; 12,000 apartment units; 60 multifamily properties.

60%

RESIDENTS of New Orleans rent, compared to 35% average nationwide (2013).

33%

INCREASE in median gross rent in New Orleans from 2004 to 2013.

$1.6 million

FUND NAME: Rental Housing Assistance

OBJECTIVE: Establish rental assistance for low- and moderate-income victims of Katrina; renovate rental units; expand availability of affordable housing.

RESULTS: Provided monthly rental subsidies to 373 families in damaged Louisiana communities, reducing financial burden and allowing hurricane victims to return home.

Healing and Caring After the Storm

The Qatar Katrina Fund's Health Care Projects

HURRICANE KATRINA devastated health-care infrastructure across New Orleans and the Gulf Coast, leaving hundreds of thousands of people stranded without access to vital medical services. The Qatar Katrina Fund helped provide immediate relief, supporting new community health centers and mobile health-care units. The fund also gave financial aid to facilities like Memorial Hospital in Gulfport, Mississippi, and Children's Hospital of New Orleans as they struggled to help the storm's victims, many of whom had no homes—and no health insurance.

Ten years later, the legacy of the fund is a better, more nimble health system. Facilities include a new network of community health centers operating in New Orleans' poorest neighborhoods and a renovated Memorial Hospital, which has just opened the first neonatal clinic in southern Mississippi.

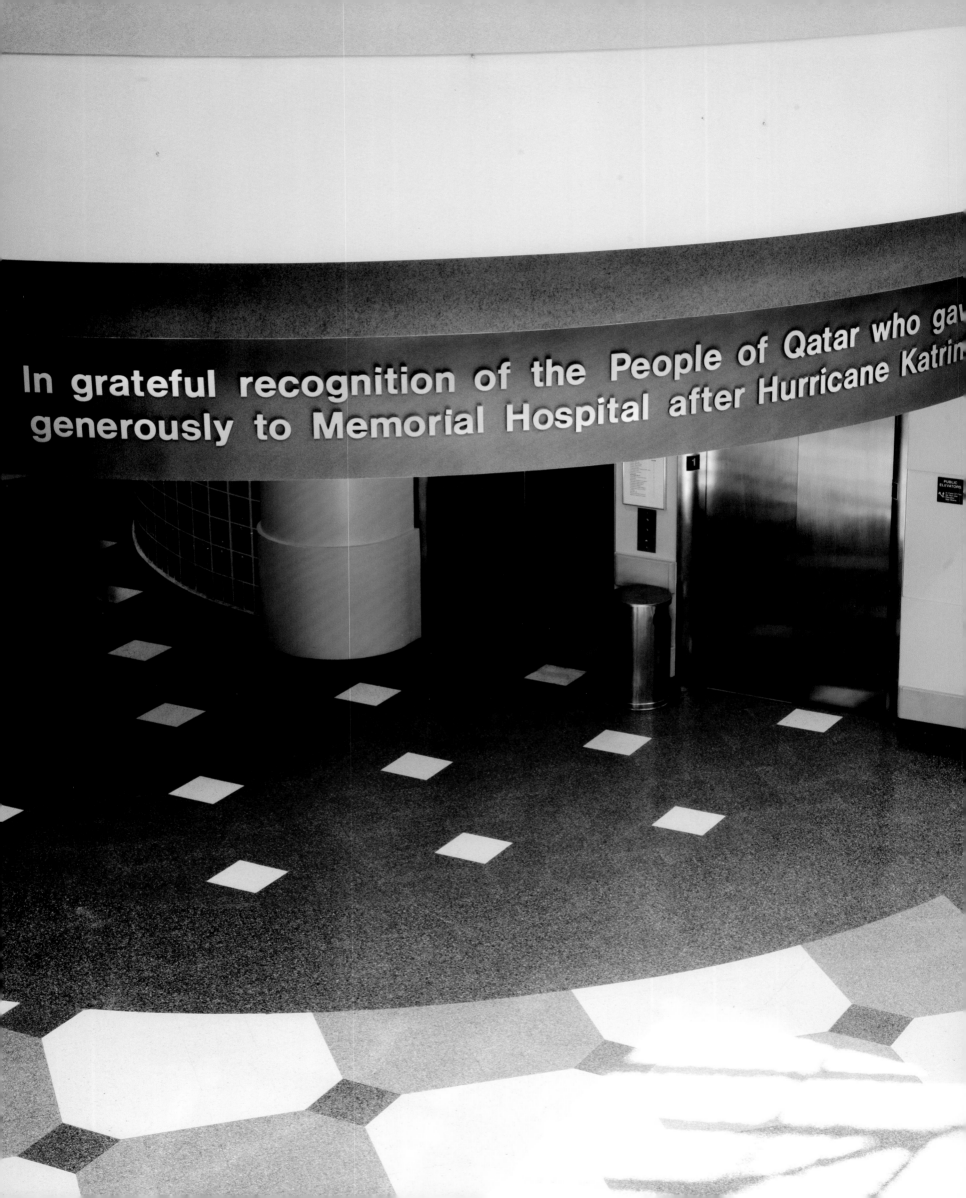

Memorial Hospital of Gulfport, Mississippi

THREE BLOCKS south of Memorial Hospital in Gulfport, Mississippi, are the railroad tracks, which follow the coast in a gentle curve for miles. Three blocks farther south is US Route 90, the coastal highway. Beyond that is a broad white-sand beach and the glittering blue waters of the Gulf of Mexico. Most days the Gulf is speckled with sailboats and shrimpers coming and going. On August 29, 2005, that same sea was a churning mass 30 feet high, and both sand and boats were being hurled far inland.

"Everything in town south of the railroad tracks was completely destroyed," says Janet Stuart, marketing manager at Memorial. "Everything in Harrison County south of the railroad tracks, actually. It was something."

> "Everything in town south of the railroad tracks was completely destroyed. It was something."
>
> **JANET STUART**, marketing manager at Memorial Hospital

< GULFPORT, MISSISSIPPI, after Hurricane Katrina hit. *Above,* Gulfport in May 2015

400 Memorial employees lost their homes in Katrina—many worked and lived at the hospital for weeks or even months afterward

Stuart lives 13 miles east of Gulfport in Biloxi, on higher ground, and didn't suffer much storm damage. But she was lucky; 400 other hospital employees lost their homes. Many of them ended up living in the hospital as it was transformed into a huge critical care hub at the epicenter of the Katrina disaster zone. If not for an exceptional grant of $10.8 million from the Qatar Katrina Fund, Memorial would have struggled to meet the urgent medical needs of thousands of patients, many of them low-income storm victims with no insurance.

"We never had to evacuate the hospital. We had our own generator," explains Gary Marchand, Memorial's president and CEO when the storm hit. Marchand lives in Long Beach, three miles from the hospital and a mile inland from the railroad tracks. "We happened to have about a 100-foot pine tree that ended up impaled into our roof in three different spots. You could walk into the house and see tree branches hanging through the Sheetrock in the foyer, water coming in through holes," he recalls. "It held the roof down and probably made sure that my wife and son were safe. I have come to believe that God put it through my roof to make sure they *were* safe. You just come to accept those bad things that happened."

Marchand was one of 620 Memorial employees on duty when Katrina struck, and he stayed at the hospital for two weeks straight. "That's when the staff realized that I needed to get out of these four walls," he says with a chuckle. He had been talking to his family on the phone and knew they were safe; he also knew the roads were impassable, but suddenly he just had to get out and see them. "That was my one emotional moment," he says. "I loaded into a military Humvee, hit this road down to my house, and all we saw was pine trees toothpicked across the road for four blocks. I told the sergeant to go back to the hospital, we aren't going to make it."

It was another five or six days before Marchand finally saw his family. "It was being together at Memorial that got us [the staff] through," he says. "Because of the extensiveness of the storm, we could only replace people as others got in. The longest-term person was there close to three months, an emergency room employee who had lost everything and was bedding down at the hospital."

In the first few weeks after the storm, Memorial was the most operational health-care asset in southern Mississippi, with power, food, pharmaceuticals, and nursing services. It quickly turned into a community shelter and hub. Hundreds of homeless locals and discharged patients camped out in an unfinished food camp, "the Village," alongside emergency workers. "Any food anyone had, we were sharing," Marchand says.

Then the volunteers began to arrive. The hospital found them beds, fed them, then sent them into the outlying communities of Mississippi and Louisiana to do their work and return for the night. Two of the hospital's units were too badly wind-damaged to be used for nursing purposes, so they were turned into makeshift dormitories. "I slept in my office for two weeks. Our nursing staff, everybody, was bedded down."

The hospital's busiest day was September 9, 2005, when 700 patients went through the emergency room. "That's still the highest ever," Marchand says. "Normally we do 225 a day. And we weren't even counting the other stuff—the State Department had dropped off tetanus shots, people had clothes or they didn't, they'd walked here, they couldn't drive. We had helicopters taking off and landing, military aircraft. We'd clear parking lots for the big Chinooks to land. They'd say, 'We picked these people off a rooftop in Hancock County' or 'We have these people on a rooftop, they need medicine,' and we'd provide that medicine."

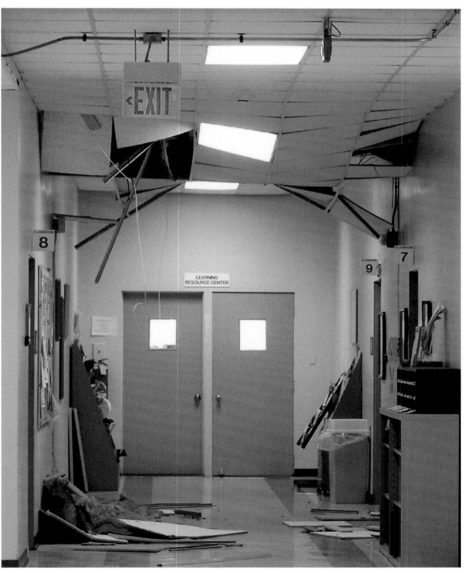

"We've advanced medicine in the state of Mississippi over the last 10 years, and Qatar is a part of that story."

GARY MARCHAND, CEO of Memorial Hospital

"It was a great time though," Marchand continues, "as painful as it was to see the physical damage. Despite all the bad memories, all the challenges … what keeps shining out of that was the good humanity that existed. Every neighbor was a good neighbor; every person had absolute compassion for everyone else. The humanity that rose in people—I'm having goose bumps thinking about it now.

"You protected someone else's property. If you had a generator, you shared it. Restaurants that had food cooked it all and gave it away—you saw signs, 'free food.' It was really incredible. To this day, I miss the humanity of that experience, I really do."

Thinking about the gift from Qatar, Marchand says, "I'm starting to get goose bumps again … It was sort of like the seed you plant in the ground that grows. It helped 1,500 individual patients; 4,500 inpatient days of care; 42,000 out-patient cares." The hospital reimbursed itself at cost, so they never profited from the transactions. They allocated $2.8 million to medical staff services, and the remainder was drawn down over two to three years for services provided to patients.

"That's $10.8 million of our own resources that we never had to use, so the gift from Qatar grew … We were able to use that money to rebuild our services." Because of the storm, Memorial became a Level II trauma center and Mississippi's first primary stroke centre. The hospital deployed its medical services farther and farther inland, following the population as it relocated.

"You have to look at how we were able to use that money. It became part of all our success," Marchand insists. "We're going to open a new neonatal facility in July, and a new adult bedded unit in August—all new, modern units. One of the seeds that allowed us to recover was that gift … The Qataris are interwoven into our success. They're part of the success of the hospital in every way.

"We've advanced medicine in the state of Mississippi over the last 10 years, and Qatar is a part of that story … We are so significantly different, by any measure, and it's because of the people that helped us recover from the storm."

Memorial Hospital of Gulfport, Mississippi

$10.8 million

FUND NAME: Qatar Hope Fund

OBJECTIVE: Cover health-care services that patients or insurance companies could not pay after Katrina.

RESULTS: Funded health care for thousands of uninsured patients affected by hurricane.

2nd

HIGHEST PERFORMING regional hospital in coastal Mississippi (*US News* ratings 2014–2015); state's first certified primary stroke center.

445

BEDS licensed to Memorial Hospital for general medical and surgical cases.

72,401

EMERGENCY ROOM VISITS (2014): 16,354 general admissions; 6,485 annual inpatient surgeries; 8,463 annual outpatient surgeries.

1946

FOUNDED by Harrison County and City of Gulfport as nonprofit medical complex.

181

PHYSICIANS, specializing in emergency medicine, women's and children's services, orthopedic services, medical rehabilitation, cardiovascular services, neurosciences, oncology.

32.2%

OF LOW-INCOME RESIDENTS had no medical insurance 2004–2006.

"It was a very generous thing to do. We were all very pleasantly surprised by their [the Qataris'] marvelous beneficence."

DR. JESSE PENCO, internal medicine specialist, Memorial Hospital

Children's Hospital of New Orleans

THE ONLY full-service hospital exclusively for children in the entire Gulf South, the Children's Hospital of New Orleans didn't suffer a lot of damage during Hurricane Katrina. Located on a gentle rise close to the Mississippi River, west of downtown, the facility is 18 feet above sea level so wasn't flooded, though it did experience some wind and rain damage.

"We had to evacuate the whole hospital because the water supply was cut," explains Cathleen Randon, director of public affairs, of that dramatic week. "We had no water for our coolers. Since then, we've put in water tanks so we won't ever have to close our doors again... There were looters in the building right away. The lawlessness in the first days was horrendous." Without other vital city services like sewage removal, electricity, and police protection, the hospital announced that it would close on the morning of August 31, two days after the broken levees had flooded New Orleans.

The evacuation was an extraordinary—and extraordinarily successful—undertaking for the hospital's 100 patients, their families, and 300 employees and medical staff. Other children's hospitals across the country and as far away as Canada offered immediate assistance. All patients were evacuated in less than 24 hours, among them 21 critically ill pediatric patients and 26 sick newborns. Children's Mercy Hospital in Kansas City sent three planes and a medical team to airlift 30 patients and their families; Texas Children's Hospital in Houston sent another two aircraft; two other hospitals sent helicopters.

At 8 a.m. on Thursday, September 1, the last two intensive care patients left for Houston in a helicopter, and Children's Hospital closed for the first time in its 50-year history. Steve Worley, president and CEO, turned out the last lights and locked the front door. He could only imagine what lay ahead—and marvel at the fact that all the patients were safe and in good hands, far from New Orleans.

The hospital reopened at full capacity six weeks later, on October 10. All 1,600 employees were called back to work, but only two-thirds returned. The remaining staff faced a huge workload, treating sick children from across Louisiana and beyond while their families struggled to rebuild after the devastation wrought by Katrina.

Many donors helped with the healing. The largest gift came in 2006: a $5.3 million contribution from the Qatar Katrina Fund. The bulk of this money was used to create the Qatar Cares Fund, to help pay for medical care not covered by insurance for children whose lives were affected by Katrina.

In the years since, Children's Hospital has worked aggressively with the medical community to preserve and improve all aspects of pediatric care, education, and research. "It has been an amazing, unbelievable time," says Randon. "And it's amazing what the city and region have done since—and because of—the storm, and thanks to gifts like the one from the Qataris."

Immediately following Katrina, Randon explains, the hospital allowed displaced private community pediatricians to see patients in its outpatient specialty clinics. "Three of our five Kids First primary care clinics—in Louisa, Canal, and Mid-City—were destroyed by the hurricane. These clinics provided primary care to the underserved population of the city. All three have since been restored. One was expanded (Prytania), and two new Kids First clinics (in Metairie and New Orleans East) have been opened. The remaining money donated by the State of Qatar enabled us to restore or renovate those much-needed clinics."

Today, Children's Hospital is a 247-bed not-for-profit medical center offering the most advanced pediatric care for children from birth to age 21. Its state-of-the-art facilities include neonatal, pediatric, and cardiac intensive care units.

"The gift from the people of Qatar was the largest gift that we have received since Hurricane Katrina, and we are deeply grateful for their generosity," Randon says. "Children's Hospital has survived the storm."

∨ **HIS HIGHNESS** Sheikh Hamad bin Khalifa Al-Thani, Amir of Qatar, meeting a young patient at the Children's Hospital of New Orleans in April 2008

"It's amazing what the city and region have done since— and because of—the storm, and thanks to gifts like the one from the Qataris."

CATHLEEN RANDON, Director of Public Affairs, Children's Hospital of New Orleans

Children's Hospital of New Orleans

247

BEDS in this not-for-profit children's medical center.

400

PHYSICIANS; over 40 pediatric specialties.

200,834

PATIENTS (2012), from all 64 Louisiana parishes, 37 states, 6 foreign countries.

150,000

CHILDREN visit one of 12 Children's Hospital clinics annually, including Kids First TigerCare (7 physicians) and Kids First Westbank (2 physicians).

6,800

ANNUAL INPATIENT admissions.

156,400

ANNUAL OUTPATIENT visits.

56,905

EMERGENCY ROOM VISITS (2014).

$5.3 million

FUND NAME: The Qatar Cares Fund and Kids First Clinic

OBJECTIVE: Help cover medical care for children affected by Katrina; repair, renovate, expand, and purchase equipment for two Kids First clinics in damaged low-income neighborhoods.

RESULTS: Supported 19,379 pediatric patient visits; Kids First clinics saw 18,282 patients.

< **AMBASSADOR AL-KUWARI**
visits a March of Dimes Mom &
Baby mobile unit, May 2015.

March of Dimes

THE CHEERFUL colors of the March of Dimes Mom & Baby Mobile Health Center provide an inviting escape from the noise and traffic on Lebeau Street in the Arabi neighborhood of New Orleans. Inside, a well-equipped facility provides the only prenatal care that many expectant mothers in this Hurricane Katrina–ravaged area will receive before giving birth.

Early in 2007, with a $3 million gift from the Qatar Katrina Fund, the March of Dimes purchased, equipped, and staffed three new Mom & Baby Mobile Health Centers. These were positioned strategically through southern Louisiana to serve communities whose traditional health-care infrastructure had been swept away by Katrina. "Until Louisiana gets back on its feet and rebuilds its health-care system," said Greg Gumbel, New Orleans native and honorary chairman of the March of Dimes Hurricane Relief Fund, "these vehicles will bring critical medical care directly to women and children."

March of Dimes, a national nonprofit dedicated to improving babies' health by preventing birth defects, premature birth, and infant mortality, worked directly with the Qatar Katrina Fund to design this project. "These mobile health centers will provide an immediate improvement in the quality of life in Louisiana," noted Qatar's then-ambassador to the United States, Nasser bin Hamad M. Al-Khalifa. "Providing mothers and babies easy access to health care is an important component of rebuilding communities. The results of this project will be felt for generations."

On a busy Tuesday in 2008, one unit's onboard staff is led by Gretchen Deeves, a certified nurse midwife with the Daughters of Charity Services of New Orleans, a March of Dimes partner. Her two colleagues briskly prepare the examination rooms and diagnostic equipment. Their first patient smiles as she studies an ultrasound image that tracks the progress of her pregnancy. She's a typical patient—most are young women between 16 and 37, about half in their first trimester. Some are new mothers with their infants.

After Katrina, when Arabi was flooded, the nearby options for prenatal care disappeared, and preterm births and other birth complications skyrocketed. "Transportation is a big obstacle to getting care," Deeves explains. "There is no obstetrician at the small local health center, and the nearest hospital that can handle deliveries is 12 miles away."

From the outside, the mobile units look like colorful minibuses, but inside they resemble regular medical offices, with private exam areas, waiting areas, nurses' stations, and an area for drawing blood. The units are equipped with fetal monitors, ultrasound, and other equipment, as well as a backup generator. The onboard staff provides initial obstetric exams, periodic revisits, maternal postpartum visits, educational and pre-conception counseling, pregnancy tests, even flu shots. If need be, they refer high-risk patients to full-service facilities. The March of Dimes also tracks outcome data to measure progress and assess local needs.

New patients are often walk-ins, but once they arrive, Deeves and her team prepare a full medical history, which will be maintained throughout the pregnancy and given to referral physicians and the hospital that will handle the delivery. Repeat visits are scheduled according to the movements of the mobile unit. Deeves proudly says that, after the first visit, "Most of our patients will be with us through full term."

The results are impressive. Of the 23 mobile unit patients who delivered in one quarter of 2008, only one delivered preterm—and that was during the stressful evacuation caused by Hurricane Ike.

Most important, Deeves says, is the fact that "without these mobile units, many of these women would receive no prenatal care at all."

"Who we really have to thank are the people of Qatar for their outstanding generosity, compassion, and commitment as world citizens."

GREG GUMBEL, honorary chairman, March of Dimes Hurricane Relief Fund

A safe, cozy place

"I HAD NO IDEA," says Rosa Bustamante-Forest. "I had been in academia. I came from the ivory tower to the streets." Bustamante-Forest is talking, of course, about the time after Hurricane Katrina, especially the three-year period starting in 2007, when she left a secure teaching post at the Louisiana State University Health Sciences Center to become a nurse and program manager for one of the March of Dimes Mom & Baby Mobile Health Centers in New Orleans.

When the storm struck, Bustamante-Forest had to leave New Orleans. Her home was not badly damaged, but like thousands of others she soon found herself commuting to Baton Rouge for work. "All any of us wanted to do was come home," she says. Then she heard about a new program looking for staff. In her university work, Bustamante-Forest had studied a new evidence-based model of prenatal care being practiced across the nation. She had imagined bringing it to New Orleans, and here was a chance. She applied and was soon managing the program.

The mobile units provided free prenatal and postpartum care to any mother and baby who came to their doors. The Qatar grant that allowed March of Dimes to buy the three units also covered all the operational costs—salaries, gas, supplies, and so on—and any medical costs not paid for by the patient's

"The unit became a safe, cozy place for women to congregate and tell their stories."

ROSA BUSTAMANTE-FOREST,

nurse and program manager, March of Dimes

insurance. If the patient had no insurance—and many didn't—a clinic and money from the grant paid the costs. "It was very nice for the patients," Bustamante-Forest says.

She describes the program as "a truly fabulous opportunity to do something really special in a state that had one of the worst perinatal outcomes in the country. It really made a difference." Many patients were recent immigrants from Latino and Hispanic communities who had come to rebuild the city and found a health-care system in disarray.

"The stars really lined up," says Bustamante-Forest. "There were three of us to each van, and we all had to have multiple skills. The driver was also a medical assistant. She drew blood, did urine tests, registered people, did the billing, interpreted." All the health workers spoke Spanish, like most of their patients.

"The program was essential at that point," Bustamante-Forest says. "The target population contributed so much to rebuilding New Orleans. We were all bilingual. They got to trust us, so through word of mouth, we just got more and more patients."

It was eye-opening to be on the front lines in a city that had been "devastated every which way," as Bustamante-Forest puts it. "Some of the women lived with 10 men in one home. They were the only woman, the cook," she recalls. "I heard stories that just broke your heart. The unit became a safe, cozy place for women to congregate and tell their stories... These were poor women facing a lot of challenges, a lot of depression, they had violence in their lives. I learned a lot about human suffering—and about women's inner strength."

"I also got to meet the [then] Amir of Qatar!" she adds excitedly, remembering when His Highness visited the city in April 2008. When the Amir asked one of the patients about her experience, she explained that she only spoke Spanish and hadn't known where to go for prenatal care because none of the regular clinics had interpreters, which scared her (and is medically dangerous). "They were so excited. She explained how grateful she was for the help she got during her pregnancy," Bustamante-Forest recalls. "It was really moving."

March of Dimes

1938

FOUNDED as National Foundation for Infantile Paralysis by President Franklin D. Roosevelt in response to US polio epidemic; renamed March of Dimes Birth Defects Foundation (1976); renamed March of Dimes Foundation (2007).

51

CHAPTERS across US, including District of Columbia and Puerto Rico.

24%

OF LOUISIANA WOMEN are uninsured at time of pregnancy.

2003

LAUNCHED Prematurity Campaign in response to rising premature birth rates.

$3 million

FUND NAME: March of Dimes Mom & Baby Mobile Health Centers

OBJECTIVE: Purchase, equip, and staff three mobile medical units to provide prenatal and early pediatric care for mothers and children affected by Katrina.

RESULTS: Supported thousands of mothers and children forced to relocate to temporary housing or relief shelters, without access to medical care or public transportation.

15%

OF BIRTHS in Louisiana are premature.

382

RESEARCH GRANTS given by March of Dimes in 2013 to help prevent and treat premature births.

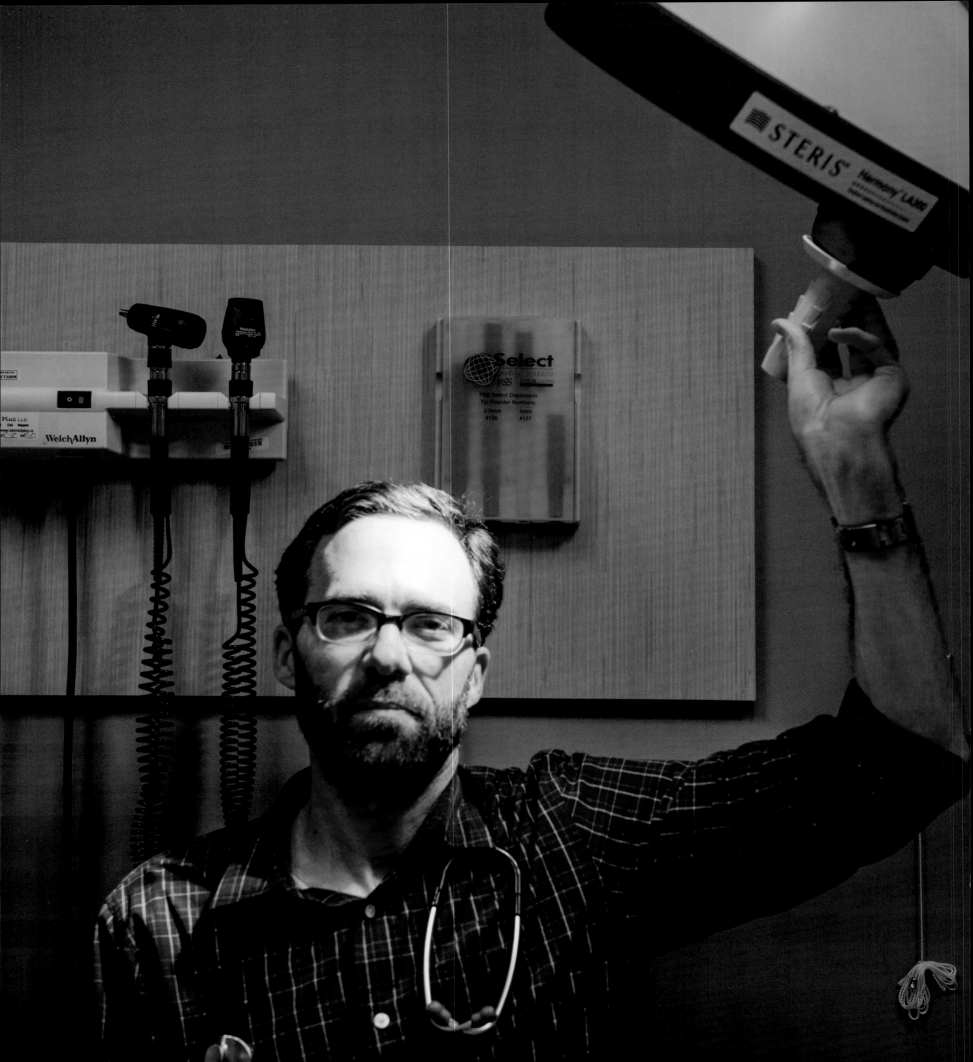

Tulane University Community Health Centers

TWO WEEKS after Hurricane Katrina, Tulane University President Scott Cowen got a phone call from a young doctor, Karen DeSalvo, head of internal medicine at the medical school. "She said, 'We are going to set up a mobile health-care unit downtown.' I said, 'Where? There's nothing there, no infrastructure.'"

Intrigued, Cowen went down to have a look. What did he see? A card table and a sign written in felt-tip pen: "Tulane Health Care Unit." A team of doctors and medical students was practicing medicine right there on the sidewalk. Most of their patients were needy, and most had no insurance.

"It was a big deal," recalls Cowen. "It was visibly important at the time, which we needed, but subsequently it's been even more important . . .

The community health centers and mobile units funded by the Qataris have revitalized health-care services in New Orleans

Because out of it grew these neighborhood clinics and mobile health-care units, and that's when Qatar came in."

The catastrophe brought on by Katrina decimated the health-care infrastructure of New Orleans. From this devastation, a new model for care delivery was born. In the extreme environment, a group of Tulane physicians came together to deliver care to first responders and people who had remained behind or returned early. They practiced in tents, shelters, police precincts, mobile vans—wherever they were needed.

The new focus was on team-based primary care located close to patients' homes, in what are known as medical homes. Instead of making people come and wait to be cared for in hospitals or emergency departments, often far from their residences, a new model arose that manages health conditions continually from a neighborhood health facility. This preventive approach tends to minimize acute health episodes and costly hospitalizations. It can now be found all over New Orleans, in more than 20 clinics run by Tulane and other organizations.

One of the first sites created after Katrina was at Covenant House, says Dr. Lee Hamm, dean of the Tulane School of Medicine. "Our faculty worked there with some residents and students. Anybody was seen. You couldn't even process things, didn't ask for anything. Before we got space and funding, they had a card table and a chair, wrote prescriptions, talked to people . . . The initial clinic was wherever the doctor was, and the willingness."

As they found permanent spaces and got more organized, donors like the Qatar Katrina Fund stepped in to expand the model. "Later, people needed to be paid," says Hamm. "It's a relatively new model of delivering primary care where you put people like social workers and dietitians and other personnel with physicians, and they work more as a team. This clinic actually reached the highest level of that certification [medical home]."

In March 2008, the Qatar grant allowed the network to purchase a mobile medical unit that could travel to communities that didn't yet have a brick-and-mortar clinic. That same year, Tulane Community Health Center New Orleans East was founded to provide health care to one of the most medically underserved areas of the city. In 2012, the original center at Covenant House reopened as the Ruth U. Fertel/Tulane Community Health Center on North Broad Street (in a renovated restaurant donated by the family of Ms. Fertel, founder of the Ruth's Chris Steak House chain).

"About a decade ago, most people began to realize that having a large central clinic doesn't provide good access," explains Hamm. "It's better to have dispersed clinics near where people live. They can drop by, especially if they don't have transportation . . . You have an appointment, you show up, you get to see the team close to that time.

"That's what's happened now throughout the city. It would be exaggeration to say Tulane was responsible for the whole transformation, but it was facilitated by Tulane's leadership."

Cowen agrees. "The money they [the Qataris] gave was the beginning of what turned out to be a robust build-out of a whole string of health-care units across the city," he says. "It was timely not just because of the disaster, but because health-care delivery was changing across America. And now New Orleans is a leader in that."

Both Hamm and Cowen stayed in New Orleans through the storm. Hamm spent a week in Tulane Hospital, helping to coordinate the evacuation of patients and staff. The downtown building was flooded, had no power or electricity,

and didn't reopen until February 2006. Two other hospitals, VA and Charity, never reopened.

But despite all the suffering it caused, Hamm says Katrina has changed the city's health-care systems in some truly positive ways. "There is a tremendous amount of new construction, a revitalization of the city," he says. "We are going to have two new major hospitals, and a transformation of the whole system of medical delivery by these clinics. So we're providing better care than prior to Katrina.

"In the long run, this sort of catastrophe does force a metropolitan area to undergo a transformation, hopefully a good one. That's probably the case in New Orleans. There's been some bumps along the road, but ultimately we're in the midst of a revitalization, a sort of renaissance for the city."

DR. KAREN DESALVO, *left,* with a Tulane Health Center patient. DeSalvo is now Acting Assistant Secretary for Health in the U.S. Department of Health and Human Services.

Tulane University Community Health Centers

21,983

LOW-INCOME PATIENTS received health care from Tulane physicians at temporary centers until community health centers built.

2008

MOBILE MEDICAL UNIT purchased to address community needs where permanent health-care facilities destroyed; Community Health Center New Orleans East founded to give underserved area access to health care.

20,000

PATIENTS served annually by Tulane Community Health Centers, at 20% annual growth rate.

$5 million

FUND NAME: Community Health Centers

OBJECTIVE: Expand and sustain Tulane University Community Health Centers; purchase mobile medical unit for neighborhoods hit hardest by Katrina.

RESULTS: Created new community health centers and mobile medical unit that provided more than 50,000 consultations with low-income patients.

90

STAFF: doctors, social workers, case managers, patient representatives, workforce training support.

8

COMMUNITY HEALTH SITES now owned and operated by Tulane University.

Coastal Family Health Center

"WE WERE still very much in survival mode," says Angel Greer about the months after Katrina, when she first joined the Coastal Family Health Center in Biloxi, Mississippi. "We had about 23 temporary locations, including tent cities and homeless shelters where we were practicing medicine. We had just started a pharmacy out of a field house, with nothing more than a cell phone." Many of the staff had lost their homes, or were trying to rebuild—and doing it in the evenings, after long hours on the front lines treating hundreds of low-income Katrina victims. "It was pretty traumatic," Greer says.

The not-for-profit Coastal Family Health Center operates a network of community health clinics across coastal Mississippi. They cover all three southern counties, from the Louisiana state line in the west to the Alabama border in the east.

< **ANTONIO TERRY**, medical assistant

"We see everyone," explains Greer, who is now Coastal Health's executive director. "But our target population, the core of our mission, is to serve the uninsured." In Mississippi, that's a sizable population. It's the poorest state in the union: close to one in four of its three million residents live below the poverty line, and about one in five have no health insurance whatsoever.

Hurricane Katrina destroyed two of Coastal Family's seven permanent clinics. It also wiped out the entire information technology and billing system, two mobile health-care units, and 60,000 medical records. The clinics were providing primary care to more than 30,000 patients a year before the hurricane, but this number ballooned afterward. And there was no let-up after the first wave of injuries had been dealt with. In the months that followed, many doctors closed their offices, never to return. "And we were also providing care for people who had come in as volunteers," adds Greer.

With a $3.4 million grant from the Qatar Katrina Fund, Coastal Family Health was able to restore primary care services for thousands of Mississippi residents beginning in September 2006. The grant covered costs for underinsured patients and staffed a mobile medical unit that reached the neighborhoods hardest hit by the storm.

"We had a million moving pieces and absolutely no money, no infrastructure, no records," says Greer. "We had to start from scratch . . . We benefited greatly from the generosity of Qatar, and the amazing amount of professional volunteers who came in to staff our clinics. A multitude of other organizations helped too: Project HOPE, Oprah's Angels, all different kinds of people and groups. It was very moving to see that."

Like so many health-care institutions severely damaged by Katrina, Coastal Family Health Center has not just recovered but come back better and nimbler than it was before. The organization now runs 10 health centers across Hancock, Harrison, and Jackson Counties, along with two mobile units, two school clinics, and a new pediatric health center in Biloxi.

"The staff and administration owe their jobs to the Qatar Katrina Fund, and many patients would not have received care without it," says Joe M. Dawsey, Coastal Health's executive director at the time of Katrina. Greer agrees: "If not for that benevolence to help us survive, and then plan and rebuild, it was difficult to imagine a future."

Coastal Family Health Center

2005

REBUILT 20 temporary locations and mobile units.

2014

30,000 MEDICAL VISITS; 10 health centers; 2 mobile units; 2 school clinics.

51%

OF COASTAL FAMILY HEALTH PATIENTS are uninsured and receive discounted medical care based on family size and income.

40

HOURS per week that mobile medical unit serves Mississippi residents.

$3.3 million

FUND NAME: Qatar Katrina Health Care Assistance Fund

OBJECTIVE: Cover health-care services that patients or insurance companies could not pay; staff a mobile health-care unit for neighborhoods hit hardest by Katrina.

RESULTS: Restored primary medical care for thousands of uninsured Mississippi residents; staffed a mobile medical unit.

"Imagine my surprise on visiting a Coastal Health Family Clinic in Bay St. Louis and afterwards being told that there'd be no charge because of [Qatar's] extraordinary generosity!"

ELLIS ANDERSON, Mississippi resident

An Education for a Better Future

The Qatar Katrina Fund's Education Projects

BEFORE KATRINA, New Orleans was known for many things—music, Mardi Gras, cuisine—but not as a college town. In fact, it is home to five major universities, one of which, Tulane University, "the Harvard of the South," is the largest private employer in the city. All of the universities were hit hard by the storm. Getting students back to class in the aftermath was a top priority for planners—one made much harder by the financial struggles faced by many students' families.

The government of Qatar has always placed a high value on education, an emphasis reflected in the Katrina Fund, which earmarked $38.2 million for educational initiatives. The lion's share of this money went to scholarships for more than 2,000 students at four major universities: Tulane, Loyola, Xavier, and Louisiana State. Separate grants funded a state-of-the-art College of Pharmacy building at Xavier University (the nation's only historically Catholic and African American university); repairs to mosques and schools serving the region's Muslim community; and a new community center in Pass Christian, Mississippi, to replace an older building completely destroyed by the hurricane.

Xavier University

"I SAID, 'Wow—I knew we had a saint that founded this place, but I didn't know she was working so hard.'" That's how Dr. Norman Francis reacted when he heard that the people of Qatar had earmarked $100 million to help groups affected by Katrina and were looking for applicants.

An elegant, soft-spoken man with sparkling eyes, Francis is inseparable from Xavier University of Louisiana, a historically black Catholic school founded in New Orleans in 1915 by Katharine Drexel, a wealthy heiress who was declared a saint in 2000. Now 84 and busy planning his retirement, Francis has been president of Xavier for an astonishing 47 years. "We come as a package," he says with a gentle laugh.

Francis was "in exile" from New Orleans after the hurricane when he heard about the Qatar Katrina Fund. Xavier applied and got not one but two grants: $5 million for scholarships and another $12.5 million to help finance the construction of a new pharmacy building, which opened in 2010 as the Qatar Pavilion. "The first grant allowed us to make close to 500 scholarships to kids in those years," he says, "which helped us

"Xavier University Building is a Testament to the Generosity of Qatar"

HEADLINE OF AN EDITORIAL

in the New Orleans *Times-Picayune,* October 12, 2010

raise enrollment, and helped a lot of kids who wouldn't have been able to come back and follow their careers."

After the levees broke, "we had five, six feet of water all over this campus," Francis recalls. "That's a lot of water." He had never left for a hurricane and wasn't planning on leaving for this one. His home was badly flooded and he ended up on the eighth floor of a downtown hotel with his wife, sister-in-law, and three grandchildren. CNN was on the same floor, "which was great—they were going out every day and giving us the story."

About 200 students were trapped in their dorms at Xavier. Staff used two boats they found on campus to ferry people about. Two cooks who worked in a convent kitchen had stayed behind, and they had freezers full of food, so everyone ate well. After three or four days, Francis says, "the army and navy started coming in and evacuating everyone . . . I got out on Thursday, when the elevators at the hotel were totally disabled. It was hot in there—man, it was hot!"

"The city was really under military control," he continues. "When we left the hotel, we had to roll up our pants and walk in tubs of iodine water. We were put on a flatbed truck. As we went down Canal Street, the looting was on. It's amazing what folks do . . . A couple of guys threw pants and shirts to the kids."

When they got to Baton Rouge, his wife asked him what room they had in the hotel. "I said, 'We got the ballroom and a blanket. Go find a place to sleep tonight!' . . . That was the experience of the hurricane hitting."

Francis set up in his hometown of Lafayette, in Cajun country, 135 miles northwest of New Orleans, and immediately started working out a way to get back. Xavier decided to reopen on January 17, 2006. "I'll never forget. I came to campus to meet with [Presidents] Clinton and Bush Senior, I think it was December 11. Clinton said . . . 'You must be crazy!' They were painting and repairing everywhere . . .

On January 17, we started classes for what was the new term." The commencement speaker for the restart was "a young guy named Barack Obama. I'd never heard him speak, but he did a hell of a job."

Three-quarters of the students came back; many others switched to colleges elsewhere, most of which waived their fees. "They went to very good schools and learned how good they had it in Xavier," Francis says.

Like the other colleges in town, Xavier was worst hit in September 2006, when freshman enrollment plunged to 450 compared to 1,000 the year before. "Families were scared to death to send students to a New Orleans that had just experienced such a disaster. By that, Katrina put the largest obstacle to our future, by losing so many students. And that hole followed through your school like a cancer. It took four years to get the numbers back.

"Qatar's generosity enhanced the university's recovery."

The Qatar Pavilion

XAVIER HAS A reputation for graduating the best African American students in the Gulf region, notably in pharmacy and premed. "When you think of all the health-care workers we graduate every year," says Francis, "you can walk into any pharmacy in New Orleans, just ask, 'What year did you graduate from Xavier?' Don't have to ask *if* they graduated from Xavier, they all did. That money from Qatar helped many of those students get their degrees."

Francis isn't just referring to the scholarships provided by the Qatar Katrina Fund. He's also talking about the extraordinary grant of $12.5 million that paid more than half the construction costs of the Qatar Pavilion, the elegant new home of Xavier's College of Pharmacy.

The college, the only pharmacy school in New Orleans, has an 80-year history of training pharmacists. After Hurricane Katrina, many pharmacists and doctors, particularly in the hard-hit African American community, left the city. In the years since, the shortage has been identified as one of Louisiana's most serious health-care problems. The new pharmacy building will allow Xavier to continue to address the health-care needs of thousands of Katrina victims, many of whom came from poor backgrounds.

"One of things we have here is a center for minority studies," explains Kathleen Kennedy, Xavier's dean of pharmacy. "It focuses on research and education, and reaches out to provide for an underserved community. That's one reason Qatar wanted to help us."

Kennedy is standing in the soaring glass atrium of the five-story, 60,000-square-foot college. "We have state-of-the-art teaching facilities, an auditorium downstairs that seats 440 students. We also have a research facility on the fourth floor with four new labs, and an animal care facility on the top floor. It amazes me every time I go up there and see it."

Before Katrina, the college had set the goal of increasing its pharmacy class to 165 students a year. "We were bulging at the seams for where these people would go," Kennedy says. "Now we've reached that number, and research has really improved, especially given the facilities we have now."

The Amir's Visit to Xavier

IN APRIL 2008, His Highness the Amir of Qatar and his daughter, Sheikha Hind bint Hamad bin Khalifa Al-Thani, came to a ceremonial ground-breaking for the Qatar Pavilion and met some Xavier scholarship recipients at a luncheon. Among them was Arian Gilyot, an accounting major whose family home in New Orleans' Lower Ninth Ward was destroyed by Katrina. The family fled to Mississippi, where Gilyot went to a community college. But she was unhappy, and asked Xavier's admissions office if there were any ways to cover the university's higher tuition fees. She applied for and got a Qatar scholarship, which allowed her to return to New Orleans and complete her studies at one of the state's best schools.

Gilyot told her story at the luncheon, struggling at times to control her emotion. "It has made a huge difference," she said, looking directly at His Highness the Amir. "From the bottom of my heart, thank you, thank you, thank you." Then she repeated her message in Arabic: "*Shukran, shukran, shukran.*"

"The first grant allowed us to make close to 500 scholarships, which helped us raise enrollment, and helped a lot of kids who wouldn't have been able to come back and follow their careers."

DR. NORMAN FRANCIS, president of Xavier University

QATAR
PHARMACY
PAVILION

Opening Fall 2009

Qatar
Katrina
Fund

An exchange with Qatar

"WE WERE the displaced people," says Dr. Sara Al-Dahir. "I graduated from Xavier right after Katrina—I was about to start my fourth and last year of pharmacy school when it hit. Then Qatar jumped in."

Al-Dahir never forgot the kindness of the Qatari people, and when she won a Fulbright Scholarship in 2010, she elected to do her exchange year at Qatar University. While she was there, two Xavier students joined her on six-week exchanges. Al-Dahir is now a professor at Xavier and oversees an exchange between the two universities.

"We just had two students who were there for four weeks," explains Kathleen Kennedy, dean of pharmacy at Xavier. "And their students come here to get a month's training. It really has set up a good exchange. Our students get to go to that country, learn about health care there, and Qatari students get to come here and work in a US hospital."

Al-Dahir is Arab American on her father's side and German American on her mother's. The family was flooded out by Katrina, and Al-Dahir found herself driving north with her widowed mother, her brothers and sisters, and her two young children. They had no money for a month—their bank had been flooded—and no clothes but the ones they were wearing.

< **DR. SARA AL-DAHIR**, *center*, with exchange students
WASSAM ELKASSEM, *left*, and **AMANDA GREGO**, *right*

> ## "I had the opportunity a year later … to meet a lot of people from Qatar. It was really nice, being able to express my gratitude."
>
> **CHELSEA HICKS**, Xavier grad and Qatar scholarship recipient

"We met some strangers on the road. They lent us their apartment in Chicago, God bless them," she says. "The kindness! They just said, 'Here is the key.'" Al-Dahir did her fourth year in Chicago, somehow finishing school on time.

She did not get a direct scholarship from Qatar, but about 20 of her classmates did. "They gave so much to the college that it was able to keep running. Their generosity meant that we were able to finish our clinical accreditation," she says.

The exchange with Qatar University is now in its fifth year. Two to three students do it in each direction each year, usually in the spring. The Qataris pay for everything except the plane tickets. "It's very, very generous," says Al-Dahir. "A lot of the students haven't got passports; they've never been to another country. They love it. We can't accept everyone that applies."

It's Nice to See a Familiar Face
Chelsea Hicks

CHELSEA HICKS IS still haunted by the ghost town that was New Orleans in the months after Katrina. A native of New Orleans East, Hicks left town with her family when the hurricane hit. She ended up in St. Louis, Missouri, only returning to begin her pharmacy degree at Xavier in January 2006.

"It was eerily unpopulated," Hicks recalls. "Luckily, I qualified for a Qatar scholarship. I used the funds to stay on campus. It was a lot more convenient. The neighboring area was still devastated, no streetlights, not a lot of stores open." There were also no restaurants, so Hicks and her boyfriend (now her husband) ate fast food every day for the first few months. "There was no place else to eat," she laughs. "It was really not healthy."

Hicks says she found it shocking, and nice, that another country halfway around the world wanted to help her city

and especially her school. "I had the opportunity a year later, when they had the ground-breaking ceremony for the new college, to meet a lot of people from Qatar. It was really nice, being able to express my gratitude," she says. "For us as students, it really did mean a lot."

When she graduated in 2009, Hicks had to move to Dallas, Texas, to find work. She enjoyed the experience but missed her family, and was happy to move back two years later. Many of her younger friends have not returned, but she says the older people won't give up on the city. "My mom, my aunt, my husband's folks, they're all still here, they love it. It's been a struggle, but things are getting a lot better."

Hicks loves her job at the Daughters of Charity clinic in New Orleans East. "We are really focused on the patients," she says. "A lot of them are indigent. They don't have any type of insurance, low income, their health is not very good. But I have lots of time to devote to counseling them. Other places just want you to fill a lot of prescriptions—we're very focused on the patients.

"A lot of the people who come into the clinic know me," Hicks adds. "I see them in the grocery store. It's nice to see a familiar face in the community."

The Spirit of Xavier
Megan Bossier

MEGAN BOSSIER WAS just about to start her second year in Xavier University's pharmacy program when Hurricane Katrina hit. She was living at home with her mother in the Gentilly neighborhood when the call came to evacuate.

"We got about three feet of water. It wasn't that bad," Bossier recalls. "But because they didn't let us go home for so long, there was mold and just disaster everywhere." For the

next month, she lived with her mother in a downtown hotel, waiting for a FEMA trailer to be installed in their driveway. Then they moved into the trailer and started putting their lives back together.

Gentilly is one of the higher parts of the city, and a lot of its residents returned. "Some had no water at all," Bossier recalls. "We all had to get together and take care of each other. There were some neighbors who couldn't come back; we kept an eye on their places." It was a terrible time, but she misses the strong sense of community, everyone sharing and helping each other.

Bossier went back to school when Xavier reopened in January 2006. She had lost pretty much everything to the water, but one of the cruelest losses was her brand-new schoolbooks. They were in the trunk of her car, which was sitting in the driveway, half submerged. "They just towed the whole lot away. I had to start again with all that stuff," she says with a resigned laugh.

When she got a letter in the mail saying she'd been awarded a Qatar Katrina Fund scholarship, Bossier remembers thinking, "Qatar? I couldn't even pronounce it. I'd never heard of it, but I thought it was amazing." The scholarship helped relieve some of the stress she felt about paying for her education. "Doing what is effectively a doctoral program all the way through with no breaks, with no social life—it was not easy!"

Bossier is now a manager at the CVS pharmacy in Kenner, Louisiana, just west of the city. She was proud to join the ranks of Xavier graduates in her family, including her mother and her great-aunt. She recently went to a funeral and had the honor of meeting the university's president, Dr. Norman Francis. She believes that the spirit of Xavier, which Dr. Francis personifies, encouraged donors like the Qatari people to support the university in a time of great need.

"We were founded because people wanted to give whatever they could financially," Bossier says, "to help people who really need it. I am so grateful to have benefited from that."

Xavier University

$17.5 million

FUND NAME: Qatar Katrina Fellowship Fund and College of Pharmacy

OBJECTIVE: Establish scholarships for students affected by Katrina; finance construction and expansion of College of Pharmacy facilities.

RESULTS: Provided scholarships to 497 pharmacy students; built new 60,000-square-foot Qatar Pharmacy Pavilion.

73%

AFRICAN AMERICAN student body.

55%

OF STUDENTS from Louisiana; out-of-state students primarily from Texas and Georgia.

87%

OF UNDERGRADS apply for financial aid; 65% receive Pell grants.

1915

ESTABLISHED as high school by Katharine Drexel (later canonized); four-year college program added (1925).

642

STAFF: 218 faculty; 424 administrative.

1,000

PHARMACY COLLEGE applications received annually.

Tulane University

"IT'S HARD to understand if you're not from here what a mark it left on everyone," says Yvette Jones. "Everyone has a story. It's like BC and AD— everything is now before or after Katrina."

Chief operating officer and senior VP for external affairs at Tulane University, Jones is speaking from her high-ceilinged office in Gibson Hall, a grand stone building just off St. Charles Avenue in the elegant Uptown area of New Orleans. "We had about $200 million in physical rebuilding," she says, pointing to the green campus out her window, framed by the dark branches of a massive oak tree. "The total loss was $650 million with equipment and so on; 85 buildings were flooded or damaged."

Often called the Harvard of the South, Tulane is consistently ranked among the top 50 universities in the United States. It has more than 13,000 students and 4,600 staff, making it the largest private employer in New Orleans. The university was severely damaged during Hurricane Katrina and was forced to close its doors for only the second time in its history—the first being the Civil War.

A new ballroom in Tulane University's student union building was recently renamed the Qatar Ballroom, commemorating the Fund's generous gift

When Tulane reopened four months later, thousands of students faced extreme financial hardship. Reviving enrollment through scholarships became an economic necessity for the students, the university, and the city. Thanks to a grant from the Qatar Katrina Fund, the university established a fund that awarded $10 million in scholarships to 180 students.

"We say it was an equal opportunity storm," Jones says. "Everybody was affected in some way." She had two houses at the time: a holiday home on the Gulf Coast and her main residence in New Orleans. The place on the coast "was just completely gone—didn't have to do any cleanup there! In New Orleans, we had fences down, roofs down, which is nothing compared to lots of people. My house was on the right side of the canal. The levee broke on the far side, but it could have broken the other way. It's just random how these things happen."

Jones grew up in Tulsa, Oklahoma, which she calls "a dull place where you would love to raise your children." But her mother's family is from New Orleans. When she was a girl, her grandmother would take her down to Bourbon Street, heart of the city's notorious nightlife. It was a warning, Jones says—this is where you'll end up if you're not a good girl—but it clearly didn't work. Even Katrina couldn't keep Jones away from New Orleans.

Jones's role in hurricane planning was to take any students left on campus to Jackson, Mississippi, to a partner university. The levees broke on moving day, and Jones found herself on the road with 650 wards: many international students, the tennis and football teams, a lot of freshmen. "The university in Jackson was really great in helping us," she says. "We got there Sunday at two in the morning. Everyone was pretty amazing about sleeping in a gym. The freshmen made new friends. I was the mother hen."

After four days, parents started arriving and the students were put on buses and planes and sent home. One of the international students had a baby, so Jones also became a godmother.

Her other job was to start planning to come back to the campus. "I had a credit card with a $1 million line. I just charged things!" she says with a laugh. "I've never been in the military, but I imagine it was like that, like being in a war. You just had to get things done." She remembers telling a helicopter to land on a football field, for instance, except it looked like a lake from the air, so they had to find another spot.

She finally returned to New Orleans in late September. "You can't imagine what it looked like," she says. "I was crying just driving through the streets. It was deserted. There were National Guard checkpoints. The devastation—it looked like it had been bombed. We pulled up here, these great old buildings were still standing, but all the usual beautiful lush green was brown. And it was hot as hell. It looked like something out of some 22nd-century kind of movie."

Against all odds, Tulane opened in January 2006. An impressive 85 percent of students returned for that semester, but then only 800 freshmen enrolled in September, half the typical cohort. "Dr. Norman Francis [president of Xavier University] called it 'Mama's syndrome.' Mamas didn't want their babies in New Orleans," Jones says. "It took a few years to get enrollment back up to where it was.

"But honestly," she continues, "the university is more beautiful now than it ever was. It sounds corny, but there is a renewal that comes out of these disasters. Tulane did have a renewal. When I look at the landscape now, everything is just so much more alive than it ever was. The buildings—the whole campus is newer, better."

The gift from the Qatar Katrina Fund helped the revitalization in several ways. One $5 million donation helped create the new Tulane University Community Health Centers; another $10 million grant provided scholarships for students affected by Katrina for up to five years. A new ballroom in the Lavin-Bernick Center for University Life, Tulane's student union building, was recently renamed the Qatar Ballroom in the country's honor.

"As I said to the ambassador and the Amir when they came," Jones says, "they've made a big difference . . . They came wanting to do something with a broader effect in the community, not just our campus."

"When I look at the landscape now, everything is just so much more alive than it ever was. The buildings—the whole campus is newer, better."

YVETTE JONES, COO and Senior VP, Tulane University

"How do you repay that?"

"IT IS JUST amazing to be part of the city as we undergo this revitalization process," says Chad Cramer, urban designer with the City of New Orleans. For 50 to 60 years, he says, things in New Orleans were pretty stagnant, but with the attention that followed the storm, all sort of processes have been kick-started. "All of a sudden, it's like a light switch was flicked on ... and on top of that, there is all the physical rebuilding."

Cramer grew up in Slidell, Louisiana, across the lake from New Orleans. After a few years in Florida, he moved back home in May 2005. "I knew when I went back to school it would be Tulane," he says, "given its reputation and location here in town. They have a joint bachelor's and master's degree in architecture, and one of best schools around." He was 27 when he started and knew exactly what he wanted to do. He just hadn't planned on a hurricane, and didn't know he'd need a scholarship from Qatar to get back on track.

The storm hit the day Cramer was supposed to start at Tulane. He and his parents went to stay with family in Birmingham, Alabama. They had no news about their house until he found an online forum where someone had gone around in a boat taking pictures. "And what did I see? There was my house under four feet of water. When I went, it looked like someone had just dumped two

loads of mud into it. There was furniture floating around, mold growing everywhere. It was just a nightmare."

Cramer was back in town three days after Katrina and started cleanup work immediately. He did all kinds of things. "If you had Bobcats or dump trucks or whatever they needed, chainsaws to remove fallen trees from streets, that sort of thing, you were put to work," he says. "Cleaning up or rescuing people stuck in the city. It was very rewarding, no matter what you were doing."

He and a friend found work getting people their FEMA trailers. "We met everyone from every demographic you can think of and heard their stories, where they went and what happened to them. It was really emotional. Often they would bring you into their house and show you where the water went. Lots of us were still in shock, I guess."

Cramer moved into a small condo in the French Quarter. In neighboring Tremé, there were people who had stayed, and he remembers them grilling up meat in the street and feeding passersby. "It was amazing to see that, just sharing

with their neighbors. My personal experience was that people were bonding together, finding a reason to share and cooperate. The media focused on a few bad incidents, but mostly it wasn't like that."

School started in January, and Cramer was so focused on work that he had no real financial plan. He says he could not have been more thankful for the Qatar scholarship. "To have someone come in and say, 'We are going to pay for your education' was just amazing . . . I remember when I got the letter saying I'd received the grant, I had tears in my eyes. I'd never met the Amir, and he's paying for my education—how do you repay that? I was so happy that they did a little ceremony for him [in April 2008]; we *did* get to meet him. At least I was able to express in person how grateful I was."

Cramer doesn't come from a lot of money, and was the first person in his immediate family to graduate from college. "There was a little bit of pride in that, and for future generations. Now my sister is going to college." He says he really tried to take on the opportunity given him by the scholarship.

There were a lot of sleepless nights, but he graduated with honors. It was a great experience, he says. "I can't say enough good things about the education I got there."

Since 2011, Cramer has worked as an urban designer for the City of New Orleans. "I'm a design guy," he explains. "I ask, what is the city going to look like in five years, ten years?" The amount of work that's being done, and still needs to be done, is breathtaking, Cramer says. When the levees broke, New Orleans lost community centers, parks, fire stations—all the infrastructure you need to maintain a major city. "So the federal government came in and helped us rebuild so much of that," he says. "Almost every school in the city had work done."

Cramer works with many departments, including the city planning commission, which recently drafted a new city zoning ordinance, a long overdue process. The whole city is waking up to new trends and standards worldwide, says Cramer. He and his boss look at any and all aspects of the city's built environment, any private or public investment that will change the city's face, and make sure they're aligned with long-term goals.

"We ask, what is the city going to look like going forward?"

I'm a Homeowner Now
JoAnna Bannon

"BECAUSE OF MY Qatar scholarship, my parents did not have to worry about my ability to support myself in the wake of all our losses from the hurricane," says Tulane business grad JoAnna Bannon. "We had the security of knowing that the next year of my education would be paid for."

Bannon is talking from her office in a car dealership in suburban New Orleans. After five years of university and another five working less than satisfying jobs, three of them

in Dallas, she's finally back in her hometown doing a job she loves. And she just bought her first house.

It's been a long road. Bannon was entering her junior year at Tulane, about to start business school, when Katrina hit. She had a number of academic scholarships, so most of her expenses were covered. "My parents didn't support me in college," she says. "It was more the other way around. I've helped them along the way." Then her parents lost their house, her mother's family lost their house, and Bannon lost her apartment. "We were all displaced," she says, still shocked at the enormity of those weeks.

It took a year of setbacks and struggle for Bannon to get back to Tulane. Being there was a huge relief. "I was excited to get back into some level of normalcy," she says. "It was an insulator from a lot of things I was coping with outside the university. A lot of students were not from New Orleans and were not directly affected by it. It's different when you have to cope with that aftermath personally, not just working for Habitat on the weekend."

She apologizes if that sounds bitter. In the years after Katrina, a lot of Tulane students threw themselves into volunteer work, which she says she finds incredibly admirable. "People from all over supporting the people around them, even a couple of helping hands could get you through," she recalls. "A lot of people felt very vulnerable. When I think about going back to Tulane, the volunteers, the Qatar donation, what it meant for the city—those things brought a sense of support and camaraderie and security that people really needed."

Bannon calls her scholarship from the Qatar Katrina Fund "the one solid, sure thing I had in those vulnerable years . . . I came from a really meager background. It moved mountains having a university like Tulane coming to me, saying they wanted to help me. The generosity of it—I just can't say enough."

> ## "A gift the size of Qatar's was an amazing gesture of kindness and a source of hope."
> **SCOTT COWEN**, Tulane University President Emeritus

Bannon had heard of the Middle Eastern country in geography class, but it really wasn't on her radar. "That they would do something so generous just felt otherworldly… It was completely phenomenal, and completely unexpected… [Katrina was] so big, it struck a lot of people down to the core, made them want to set everything back to normal. They wanted to see the city come back better than ever, and the Qatar Katrina Fund was part of that."

Bannon graduated in December 2007, and it took her five years to land a job she really likes. She spent three years in Dallas working for an online travel agency before moving back to New Orleans in 2012. "It was all a ladder, all steps towards having a stable and coherent employment career path and professional history," she says. "Tulane does a really good job of preparing grads for the real world, supporting them so they can turn a degree into a career."

So is she happy to be back in New Orleans? "Absolutely! As much as I got to travel a lot when I worked for [the travel agency] … it all just made me homesick. I didn't realize until I spent three years away, New Orleans has a spirit and a soul that a lot of places don't. They are just streets and buildings. They have their history, but it's not the same. New Orleans is just so convoluted and eccentric. I was so glad to move back to something familiar.

"It's my home. And I'm a homeowner now."

A Source of Hope
Scott Cowen

RETIREMENT ISN'T SLOWING Scott Cowen down. In July 2014, the New Jersey native stepped down after 16 years as president of Tulane University, but not before publishing a best-selling book, *The Inevitable City: The Resurgence of New Orleans and the Future of Urban America,* the month before. He's been touring ever since, talking about the lessons of the last extraordinary decade, in which he got Tulane back on its feet after the near-fatal events of Hurricane Katrina.

"Writing the book was a therapeutic process," Cowen says from his office on Poydras Street in downtown New Orleans. Office towers and the Superdome are visible out the window. An early-morning fire is burning across the street; smoke and sirens fill the air.

"I had a desire to get this out of my system," Cowen continues. "The book's done so much better than I imagined… People all over the country have been interested because the subject, urban decay and renewal, interests everyone. It applies to places like Detroit, obviously, but also to New York, Chicago, LA."

Cowen has an impressive CV. A college football player, he spent three years in the army before getting his doctorate in finance and management. He then spent 23 years in Cleveland teaching management at Case Western Reserve University before coming to Tulane in 1998. He has published more than a hundred journal articles and four previous books, sits on many boards, and has received eight honorary doctorates. In 2009, he was given a $500,000 Carnegie Corporation Academic Leadership Award for his leadership after Katrina. He dedicated the money to Tulane's community-related activities, including the Cowen Institute for Public Education Initiatives.

Many people equate the renewal of New Orleans with the reopening of Tulane in January 2006, just four months after Katrina flooded 70 percent of its Uptown campus. They all agree that the venerable institution would never have reopened so quickly if not for the determination of its president—and he hands much of the credit to supporters like the people of Qatar.

> ## "The volunteers, the Qatar donation...those things brought a sense of support and camaraderie and security that people really needed."
>
> **JOANNA BANNON**, Tulane graduate and Qatar scholarship recipient

"A gift the size of Qatar's was an amazing gesture of kindness and a source of hope, to know that there were people around the world who cared about what was happening in the Gulf Coast, and the city, and the state," says Cowen.

Tulane is the largest private employer in New Orleans. Getting it up and running again brought 9,000 students and another 6,000 full- or part-time employees back into downtown, encouraging other businesses to follow. Some painful restructuring followed, but as he details in *The Inevitable City,* Cowen believes the rebuilding process has made Tulane a better university—and New Orleans a better city. One example is the new Center for Public Service, which made community work a requirement for Tulane undergraduates. "We wound up putting an army of students into the fabric of New Orleans, first rebuilding, now strengthening the city," he says.

"It's not just Tulane. New Orleans has changed dramatically in the last 10 years. The whole culture of the city has changed to one of innovation and creativity, citizen empowerment. We actually believe we can make a difference, working on things individually or collectively. There's been a whole sea change here... It's had a dramatic, positive impact on education, ethics reform, the criminal justice reform, the fortifying and strengthening of flood protection systems, the rebuilding of our neighborhoods—so many things."

There is still much to do. Cowen cites the appalling statistics: child poverty is still at 39 percent, with 27 percent of all people living in poverty. And there's a big issue with disconnected youth, half of whom don't have a high school education. "Eighteen percent of 16- to 24-year-olds have no job. Not surprisingly, that's where most of the crime comes from... We're still a work in progress. We can't declare victory yet."

Population numbers tell another part of the story. From 480,000 before Katrina, the city is now home to almost 380,000 people. "That's 100,000 more than five years ago, but we're still 100,000 short." The demographics have changed too. There are more Latino and Asian residents, for instance, and slightly fewer African Americans. "And we've seen a distinct increase in young people with a college education coming in," says Cowen. "They see opportunities here to start their own businesses, and companies are bringing in satellite offices—the big one is the GE central technology office," which brought 300 jobs to downtown.

Cowen hosted a dinner at the presidential residence when the Amir of Qatar came to New Orleans in April 2008. "I remember His Highness very fondly," he says. "He was very friendly, very accessible, very warm... They did a wonderful thing for the Gulf Coast region and Tulane University. They were always very gracious and never asked anything in return."

Cowen said he was impressed by how rigorous the vetting process was for the Qatar Katrina Fund. "It was competitive, vetted by a distinguished panel. It felt fair. Anyone could make their case, and receive a grant if it was impressive.

"I feel we owe the Amir and all those who helped us our thanks," Cowen adds. "Education is one of the building blocks of a democracy, a pathway out of hopelessness, and we were in a time of hopelessness. Investing in education is the great equalizer. It can bring people together. I believe it was an extremely wise investment.

"There's a word we use here, *lagniappe.* It's a Creole word that means a little extra," says Cowen. "Like when you get a baker's dozen, that thirteenth doughnut, that's lagniappe. Qatar was our lagniappe. And it was a lot more than a little bit extra, too!"

Tulane University

1834

FOUNDED as Medical College of Louisiana; merged with University of Louisiana (1847); emerged as private university (1884).

4,670

STAFF: 1,180 faculty; 3,490 administrative.

13,531

STUDENTS: 8,353 undergraduate; 5,178 graduate or professional.

10

SCHOOLS: architecture, business, continuing studies, engineering, law, liberal arts, medicine, public health, science, social work.

$10 million

FUND NAME: Qatar Tulane Scholars Fund

OBJECTIVE: Revive enrollment at Tulane by providing full scholarships to students most affected by Katrina.

RESULTS: Provided 180 scholarships to students in Louisiana, Alabama, and Mississippi who suffered losses from hurricane.

85%

OF STUDENTS RETURNED to finish school year after Hurricane Katrina.

19th

RANKING on *Newsweek* magazine's list of country's 25 "most service-minded schools."

Loyola University

"THE UNIMAGINABLE happened." That's how Christopher Wiseman describes Hurricane Katrina, which brought Loyola University to its knees 10 years ago. A native of New Orleans and a Loyola grad, Wiseman had come back to work at the university in 2004, barely a year before the storm. Nowadays he's associate VP for development, with an elegant office in Greenville Hall, a historic mansion fronted with palm trees on Loyola's verdant Broadway campus. But his first few years at the university were "pretty unsettling," to put it mildly.

Loyola is a private Catholic university, one of the largest and most prestigious in the South. Founded as a Jesuit college in 1849 and chartered as a university in 1912, Loyola is spread over two campuses on either side of St. Charles Avenue in New Orleans' affluent university district. It is open to students of all faiths, and is particularly known for its law school and its music programs.

Loyola didn't flood during Hurricane Katrina, unlike neighboring Tulane University. Though Loyola is closer to the Mississippi River,

The main damage, Wiseman says, was more insidious: people watching the events unfold on CNN and Fox News no longer wanted to send their children to college in New Orleans. Despite the best efforts of city, state, and university officials to convince people that the city was returning to normal, the rumors of lawlessness, toxic waste, and impending cholera epidemics were hard to shake. In January 2006, 91 percent of students from the fall 2005 cohort returned, but by the following September enrollment was in freefall.

"There was an effort to recruit students who knew they were in a recovering city," explains Wiseman. "They came in eyes wide open. We recruited a lot of people who wanted to help in the recovery of New Orleans. We had hundreds of students literally helping to gut homes, rip out the damaged walls, and install Sheetrock . . . It is an explicit part of our mission as a Catholic university. We want to graduate students who want to live a life of service."

The spirit of altruism that followed Katrina had a profound effect on the university, says Wiseman. "Tutoring is big now, working with schools . . . It changes you for the good, that kind of service. A huge number of our students now do service work in the community."

At the time of the storm, more than half of Loyola's students came from out of state. "In some ways that was a blessing," says Wiseman. "Those students could go back to their hometowns and enroll in a school there, so they dispersed to hundreds of schools across the country. All but one of the 28 Jesuit universities in the United States took students in. They said, 'Your Loyola tuition is good here.'"

The remaining students weren't so lucky. They came from the three states most affected by the hurricane—Mississippi, Alabama, and Louisiana—and many were in danger of having to discontinue their studies because of the financial

it sits on higher ground than Tulane, which was inundated with water from Lake Pontchartrain to the north. "The floodwaters stopped a few blocks short of our campus," says Wiseman, "so we were lucky. Though we did have damage from above, in the low millions [of dollars], the wind tearing off roofs, rain getting in, that sort of thing." The university had no power or water for more than two months, so some professors' research was affected, and many valuable items were damaged or lost.

hardship Katrina had caused them and their families. With the grant from Qatar, Loyola established the Qatar Loyola Scholarship Fund to provide monetary assistance to affected students.

The gift from Qatar helped Loyola on two fronts, Wiseman explains. "It gave families directly affected by the storm the opportunity to not throw away their dream of a college education. And for the institution, it gave us a way to restore enrollment, so we could rebuild and remain sustainable."

Wiseman was impressed by the Qatar Katrina Fund's thorough accounting process. They came down a few times and went through the books, he says, to make sure all the money was being spent correctly. Then they had PricewaterhouseCoopers, one of the Big Four international auditors, go through all the accounts. "We really appreciated the rigor. It showed they really cared the money was going to the right people, that it was really helping people."

A few students who benefited from the scholarship fund got to meet the Amir of Qatar at an event held at Tulane University in April 2008. "There were a couple of hundred people, a receiving line. He shook hands with some students," Wiseman says. There was a lot of gratitude on display, he recalls. "Some of those kids will tell you, they couldn't have come to Loyola if it wasn't for the Qatar scholarship."

One of the fascinating effects of Katrina, Wiseman reflects, is the way that the levee failures committed or recommitted so many people to the city. In the years since the storm, he has watched thousands of volunteers, many of them high school students, come to town to help rebuild. Many end up staying or decide to attend college in the city.

"I have a good friend from San Francisco, a high school teacher," he says with a laugh. "She did that—came to do volunteer work and brought her kids. She went back but they ended up coming to school here, just because they love it."

"The gift from Qatar gave families directly affected by the storm the opportunity to not throw away their dream of a college education. And it gave Loyola a way to rebuild and remain sustainable."

CHRISTOPHER WISEMAN, Associate Vice President for Development, Loyola University

"I will always be eternally grateful"

"I'M BLESSED, I know that," says Jauné Jackson. The young journalist and Loyola grad is taking a coffee break from her dream job, producing the 5 p.m. news for the New Orleans affiliate of NBC. She's thinking about Hurricane Katrina and how a scholarship from the other side of the world shaped her future.

"I'm truly blessed," Jackson repeats. "I didn't lose any family members. We lost a house, but that's replaceable. We actually slept one night in the parking lot of a park, but we were safe. I can't complain."

When the storm hit, Jackson was just about to start her senior year of high school. The family drove away from their home in New Orleans East on Sunday, August 28, the day before the levees broke. "There was no way to go back," she recalls. Both her parents had lost their jobs, and every school in her hometown was closed. After a few weeks in a hotel in Texas, they went to Houston, where Jackson did a semester of schooling.

Houston was a big culture shock. "In New Orleans, everyone knows everyone. In that public school in Houston, there were 700 kids in senior class." Thinking back on it now, Jackson says Katrina helped her grow. "It was a blessing. I was exposed to a place where I'd never been before, a totally different world only six hours away."

> ## "[Qatar is] a very small country, and to hear that they just felt they had to do something to help us, it's amazing."
>
> **JAUNÉ JACKSON**, Loyola grad and Qatar scholarship recipient

That said, the family went back to New Orleans as soon as they could, in January 2006, to a rental property belonging to Jackson's grandparents. "A shotgun house," she explains. "My mom and my dad and two sisters on one side, my grandparents on the other. We were so grateful to my family for making that sacrifice."

Jackson always wanted to work in journalism but hadn't decided on television or print. She was accepted into Loyola's broadcast journalism stream for fall 2006; then, in a major post-Katrina restructuring, the university cut the program. "That was another roadblock," she chuckles. "They said I could still go, but my concentration would be print. And I was able to get an internship at a TV station, which I loved."

Paying the tuition wasn't easy. Jackson got scholarships and government grants and did a work/study placement, which paid a little. Then the financial aid office told her she'd received a large grant from the Qatar Katrina Fund.

"It was almost like, huh?" she says. "A lot of us had got scholarships from different individuals donating money, but a country way across the world? I'd never heard of Qatar. Now I know it's a very small country, and to hear that they just felt they had to do something to help us, it's amazing. I will always be eternally grateful."

After working at other jobs, Jackson landed her first position as a news program producer at WDSU-TV, Hearst-Argyle Television's NBC affiliate in New Orleans. She started out on the morning newscast, doing the overnight shift. Then the producer of the 5 p.m. news show left. "The opportunity came for the job, so I went through the application process and got the position," she says proudly.

Now, a decade after the biggest news event in recent New Orleans memory almost derailed her life, Jackson is behind the cameras, making news herself.

The Kindness of Strangers
Christina Luwisch

"NEW ORLEANS IS not an easy place to get over," says Christina Luwisch, a Loyola grad who now works for the university's College of Law. "You fall in love with the people, the food, the music . . . I've traveled, but I love New Orleans and will always come back. You need some spice. Anywhere else just seems bland."

Luwisch had her love for her hometown severely tested during Hurricane Katrina. But like many natives, she's proud to have returned and rebuilt. Her mother's family is Italian, with roots in the city that go back three generations; her father is a more recent arrival. Luwisch herself was born and raised in Metairie, 15 minutes outside the city.

The family had lived through plenty of hurricanes, but none like Katrina. "We always played Russian roulette with the storms," Luwisch says. They finally evacuated on Saturday, August 27. Luwisch recalls coming out of a movie downtown and seeing that she had 17 missed calls. She ran home, packed an overnight bag, and piled into the car with the whole family, including the dog. Eight hours later, they were in Texas, where they stayed for six weeks.

Luwisch was overwhelmed by the reception there. "People wanted to buy your lunch, give us gift cards, bring us food. That was always so encouraging, the kindness in strangers." By then, the family knew that their house had been flooded out—the canals surrounding it had overflowed—but they moved back as soon as they were allowed.

Was that a hard decision? "Honey, we were coming back. No way we would ever leave this city. We had family in Chalmette [an eastern neighborhood] that had worse damage than we did. It was never a discussion."

Luwisch describes Metairie after the storm as "the weirdest thing ever… If you've ever seen a desert after a rainstorm, all cracked mud, that was what the neighborhood looked like—dried mud that cracked when you stepped on it." The family's house was green with mold blooms. "It was almost beautiful in a twisted way." The stink was horrendous, but it was home nonetheless. The house was structurally sound, and they were grateful to have the opportunity to rebuild.

The family spent the next year in the grandparents' house—"nine of us together, and the jumbo bulldog"—rebuilding. Meanwhile, Luwisch managed to finish high school and applied to Loyola. She had considering going out of state, but says she "knew what a wonderful school it was. Everyone is so kind. It's a very family-like atmosphere. When everything was so terrible, that was what I needed."

Except she wasn't sure she could afford it. She had got into college—the first in her family to do so—landed one scholarship, done everything right, but still she might be unable to go. With all the family's financial resources being funneled into rebuilding, she couldn't ask her parents for money. "They were already so overwhelmed by everything. They'd just lost their house."

Luwisch talked to Loyola's financial aid office. "That's when they told me, 'We have these Qatar funds. You might be able to qualify,'" she recalls. "And before I knew it, everything had worked out. I had the money. It was spread out over three years… It was exactly what I needed at that moment. It took that pressure off, which was looming over me. Then I started to think, maybe everything else will resolve itself too."

Receiving the Qatar scholarship reminded her of the kindness of strangers in Texas. "How do a group of people so far away decide to help people across the world, individuals

who are struggling?" she still asks herself. "That someone in another country that I'd never met would decide to help me, it was just astounding. Maybe they don't know me, but they made a profound impact on my life and the life of my family. It was really overwhelming,.. a complete life changer."

Benefiting from this generosity changed Luwisch's perspective on life. After she graduated, she became assistant director of the Gillis Long Poverty Law Center, part of the Loyola College of Law. Now she spends her time helping other students get internships or get into programs that can help them repay their loans.

"That someone in another country that I'd never met would decide to help me, it was just astounding . . . they made a profound impact on my life and the life of my family. It was . . . a complete life changer."

CHRISTINA LUWISCH, Loyola graduate and Qatar scholarship recipient

> "New Orleans is . . . not like anything else around it—and that's the way we like it. You don't appreciate what you have until you leave."
>
> **MIA BORDERS**, Loyola grad and Qatar scholarship recipient

"You're inspired by that kindness," Luwisch says. "It makes you want to pay it forward, show that same support to your community. Loyola was so kind to me, gave me a great education. Now my job allows me to do that to other people, which is great."

Luwisch coordinates programs for Loyola students and alumni attracted to public interest law. The center runs a summer internship program, for example, which places students in legal assistance offices across the country. "These are people who want to help other people and get experience. And they get a stipend of $5,000, while the firms get someone to work for them for free for a few months. It's win-win for everyone.

"There are still lots of needy people in New Orleans, and they can receive assistance from these offices," Luwisch says with pride. "If I can help with that, I will."

Falling in Love Again (with New Orleans)
Mia Borders

"FUNKY ROCK AND soul, I guess you'd call it," says Mia Borders when asked to describe her music. The Loyola grad has just finished playing at New Orleans' annual French Quarter Festival and is getting ready to take her band to Jazz Fest. "The festivals never end in this town," she says with a chuckle. "I have a four- or five-piece band, depending on the scale of the event."

Borders was born and raised in New Orleans, near the city's two most prestigious universities, Tulane and Loyola. In August 2005, when Katrina hit, she was just starting a year off after boarding at a private high school in Connecticut, then had plans to go to film school in Savannah, Georgia.

"I did take a year off. I sort of had to," she explains, "though Katrina meant I didn't spend it the way I'd envisioned. I moved back to New Orleans to clean up stuff and see what we could salvage."

The family home, where Borders had been raised by her grandmother, was flooded by about four feet of water. Most New Orleans houses don't have basements, which helped; the family was living upstairs and using the ground floor for storage. "We lost some old books and pictures, but nothing we were using on a daily basis," Borders says. "Of course, we were sad to lose that stuff, but we were very, very lucky."

After half a year of cleaning up after Katrina and falling back in love with her hometown, Borders started to re-evaluate her options. Georgia and film school suddenly didn't seem so appealing. Then her brother asked if she'd like to join a band with some musician friends. She'd always loved music and decided to give it a try. "We did our first show April 2006, so my plans shifted around music," she recalls. "I dropped the film school idea and decided to go to Loyola."

There was a lot of scholarship money available to encourage local students to stay in New Orleans, and Borders was able to get most of her tuition covered. Her largest scholarship came from the Qatar Katrina Fund. "I was very surprised," she recalls. "But I was very, very grateful."

Borders has always loved writing poetry and essays, and wound up getting a four-year English degree. She continued to play music, gigging as regularly as she could while still in school. When graduation neared, she decided to try to make a living as a full-time musician.

"I could have gone to law school or continued with my part-time job, but I was confident enough in my management team and my band that I felt we could play regularly enough to make it." A brave choice? "Yeah, or stupid, depending on how you look at it!"

She is being coy. Borders has now released two EPs, five LPs, and one live album, and has played every place worth playing in New Orleans and many farther afield, including the Kennedy Center for the Performing Arts in Washington, DC. The *Times-Picayune* described her as "confident and cool," *USA Today* called her music "deeply funky," and New Orleans' own *OffBeat Magazine* praised her for her "great music and great intensity."

Borders says her English degree has helped her develop as a songwriter, in terms of writing and framing stories. She also befriended a fair number of music school kids at Loyola,

which is famed for its music programs, including those offered through the prestigious Thelonious Monk Institute of Jazz Performance.

"New Orleans is a small world," Borders says. "It's very isolated, not like anything else around it, and that's the way we like it. You don't appreciate what you have until you leave."

She's referring both to her high school days in Connecticut—"it was cold, the food was so bland"—and to more recent forays on the road with her band. Now she's back in New Orleans, getting ready for Jazz Fest, helping bring the music back to the city where jazz was born.

Loyola University

1718

JESUIT MISSIONARIES, among earliest settlers of Louisiana, arrived with French colonizers Iberville and his brother Sieur de Bienville, who founded New Orleans in same year.

1849

FOUNDED as College of the Immaculate Conception; reopened as Loyola College (1904); chartered as university (1912).

640

STAFF: 410 faculty; 240 administrative.

4,496

STUDENTS: 2,854 undergraduate; 807 graduate; 124 doctoral; 611 law; 100 continuing education.

$1.4 million

FUND NAME: Qatar Loyola Scholarship Fund

OBJECTIVE: Provide scholarships to students directly affected by Katrina.

RESULTS: Provided scholarships to 184 students affected by hurricane; some scholarships for multiple years.

5

COLLEGES: business, humanities and natural sciences, law, music and fine arts, social sciences.

75

DEGREES: 65 undergraduate degrees; 10 graduate and professional programs.

Louisiana State University

"THERE WAS a lot of wreckage and fallen debris in Baton Rouge," says Sean O'Keefe. "It rained to beat the band. The winds were ferocious. It would have been considered a significant hurricane by any standard were it not completely eclipsed by what happened in New Orleans, which was of Homeric proportions."

O'Keefe was chancellor of Louisiana State University (LSU), one of the largest and most diverse universities in the South, when Hurricane Katrina hit. LSU's main campus, in Baton Rouge, Louisiana's capital and second-largest city, sits on a high plateau above the Mississippi, 80 miles upriver from New Orleans. It was badly battered by the storm but had no flood damage. Both the city and the campus were soon overwhelmed with displaced people, including students from colleges and universities across Louisiana and neighboring states, seeking refuge from the turmoil.

> "I was blown away that the Qatar government had even been thinking about things like this . . . It was extraordinary."

SEAN O'KEEFE, former Chancellor, Louisiana State University

To help these students continue their education, LSU enrolled 2,700 of them within days, and hundreds more over the following months. Many of the dislocated students, and hundreds already enrolled at LSU, were badly in need of financial assistance to continue their studies. The Qatar Katrina Fund provided relief by giving $3.3 million in scholarships to 1,367 students.

Baton Rouge had no electricity for the better part of two weeks; even the city's main hospital went dark. "Part of the

reason we were such a sought-after location for the diaspora was that we had a cogenerating plant," says O'Keefe. "It kept enough electricity going that we were back in business faster than anyone else . . . All those students from New Orleans who wanted to re-enroll there had an opportunity to establish some sort of normalcy in a period of massive disruption and chaos."

LSU opened its doors and admitted any student from a university in New Orleans that was closed. "And that was all of them," says O'Keefe. They didn't charge any tuition, and they tried to house everyone and provide them with meal plans. "It got a little tight," O'Keefe says with a chuckle. Some people got a room, then invited their homeless families, and their pets too. "There were some very cozy settings, that's for sure."

Speaking of pets, LSU has a veterinary college and a school of agriculture, which got together and offered to house displaced people's domestic animals. "People started coming up here; they couldn't stay in hotels because they didn't want to leave their animals," explains Bunnie Cannon, LSU's executive director of institutional advancement. "We set up a place where they could leave their pets and come and check on them every day."

This community service soon turned into a huge menagerie. "Cats and dogs are one thing," recalls O'Keefe, "but wow, there were thousands of pets, at the vet college as well as in big areas with fences, covered buildings—snakes, pet pigs, parrots!"

LSU was also home to a larger, more extraordinary medical facility, a vast acute care field hospital. With all the hospitals in New Orleans forced to close, LSU offered to house about 1,000 evacuated patients in a converted basketball arena, the 13,000-seat Pete Maravich Assembly Center. They pulled up the floor, laid out rows of cots, and filled the place up. "There were lines of hundreds of people at all hours, waiting for basic things like rehydration," says O'Keefe. "It went on for weeks, turned into something we were able to do 24 hours after it hit critical proportions."

"The city as a whole just blew up," says Cannon. "The infrastructure went crazy. An estimated 500,000 people moved here from New Orleans after Katrina. The traffic was bad enough before, but now! There were a ton of people that never went back."

O'Keefe says it took the better part of a year before LSU started to return to normal—though he thinks the university and Baton Rouge, like New Orleans, were permanently changed by the events triggered by Katrina, both positive and negative. One of the more uplifting responses, he says, was the volunteering he witnessed at the acute care facility.

"The doctors had figured out shifts for medical professionals, and people were coming from all over to volunteer," he says. "The folks that were most impressive were the students. They would show up and sit in the bleachers of the stadium, and wait to be called to assist in different areas. Hundreds of them sat there very stoically, waiting to help, waiting for someone to say, 'I need 10 people to empty bedpans.' And they'd do it, at two o'clock in the morning.

"It was the most astonishing display of humanity, of care for other people, that I'd ever seen," O'Keefe says. "And many of them were the same people that had been forced out of their homes, their campuses. Holy catfish, I'd recognize them, waiting for someone to tell them to pull a cot or change some sheets. After that, I didn't have any doubt about what the future of public service would look like."

O'Keefe was born in California, but his parents were from New Orleans, which he always thought of as the family home. Now a professor of management at Syracuse University, he has had a distinguished career as an administrator: he's been chairman of Airbus, secretary of the Navy, administrator of

NASA, and a member of the board of directors of DuPont. He first heard about Qatar's offer of help to LSU from a colleague from his days in the Reagan White House. "She called me out of the clear blue sky . . . It was amazing. I was blown away that the Qatar government had even been thinking about things like this. We were most grateful for their generosity. It was extraordinary."

O'Keefe believes that the communal spirit of Katrina—the generosity he saw in the Qatari donation and in those volunteers in the field hospital—has changed a generation. "It was staggering," he says. "It was on display then, but I believe it is still very much alive in all the people that were affected by the events. It's just not all on evidence as it was so richly at that time. Because of the generosity of folks that had no inkling of what this was about . . . it's very impressive."

Louisiana State University

$3.3 million

FUND NAME: Katrina Student Relief Fund

OBJECTIVE: Establish fund for students in financial need after Katrina.

RESULTS: Provided 1,367 scholarships to students for tuition and room and board during their degree.

1853

FOUNDED as Louisiana State Seminary of Learning and Military Academy in Pineville; forced to close because of Civil War (1861).

1870

RE-ESTABLISHED in Baton Rouge after the seminary burned down in 1869, and renamed Louisiana State University.

29,000

STUDENTS: 24,000 undergraduate; 5,000 graduate.

26%

OF LOUISIANA'S baccalaureate graduates are from LSU; 22% of master's graduates; 53% of doctoral graduates.

194

DEGREES, including 72 bachelor's and 54 doctoral; 221,000 degrees awarded (since 1869).

2,700

DISPLACED STUDENTS temporarily accepted at LSU after Katrina.

Humanity First USA

"IT WAS an experience, going through that," says Bashir Shams modestly. "I was in New Orleans and Mississippi. There was lots of damage."

Born in Pakistan, Shams immigrated to the United States in 1972. He was living in Hattiesburg, Mississippi, where he owned and operated seven Burger King restaurants, when Katrina devastated the town in August 2005. His businesses and his home were badly damaged. While struggling to deal with the disaster, Shams was also volunteering with Humanity First USA to repair other infrastructure the storm had left in tatters. He soon found himself project manager of the Humanity First Qatar-Katrina Project, established with a gift of $1 million from the Qatar Katrina Fund.

Humanity First USA is the American chapter of Humanity First International, a nonprofit organization established in the UK in the early 1990s to help underdeveloped and vulnerable communities around the globe deal with natural disasters. The organization's staff are all unpaid volunteers, mostly professionals with expertise in the business,

health-care, and education sectors. Humanity First USA is active in 19 countries worldwide. Hurricane Katrina was its first disaster on US soil.

Katrina damaged many buildings that serve the Muslim community in Greater New Orleans. For many months, religious services and classes were either halted or held on a limited basis. The Qatar Katrina Fund collaborated with Humanity First USA to repair six religious places. It was urgent work, critical to ensuring that residents felt comfortable enough to return to their battered communities and join in the rebuilding.

"None of the damage was catastrophic," says Shams. "Some of the mosques had water inside. The mosque in Kenner had some damage to the dome also. The water didn't come inside the building, but a lot of renovations needed to be done. We did a lot of work, really improved the facilities."

Shams says the renovations, begun in 2006 and completed over two years, were great for the community coming

back to the Gulf Coast after the storm. "Qatar was very generous. It was very thoughtful of them, and very timely."

In January 2007, at an honorary ball in New Orleans, Nasser bin Hamad M. Al-Khalifa, then Qatar's ambassador to the United States, was recognized by Humanity First USA for his relief work for Katrina victims. Munum Naeem, the charity's executive director, also praised the work of all the volunteers who helped with the Qatar-sponsored project, including lawyers Ricky Crisler and Amjad M. Khan and architect Geoffrey Hartnett. Naeem stressed that all Humanity First members, including many such top-notch professionals, worked on a volunteer basis.

In his speech, Al-Khalifa emphasized the need for all people to help each other during times like Katrina. In the spirit of peace and brotherhood, he recognized the efforts of the local community to renovate their properties and complimented Humanity First USA for its selfless efforts.

Humanity First USA

1994

REGISTERED in UK as Humanity First, a charity.

43

COUNTRIES now home to Humanity First chapters.

90%

OF FUNDS RAISED by Humanity First go towards humanitarian projects.

10

MUSLIM CONGREGATIONS in New Orleans, serving 5,272 residents.

25,000

SQUARE FEET of class, gym, and multipurpose space in new Islamic School of Greater New Orleans.

$1 million

FUND NAME: Repair of Religious Places in Greater New Orleans

OBJECTIVE: Repair religious places heavily damaged by Katrina.

RESULTS: Restored and reopened three mosques and three schools, allowing Muslim residents to return to their communities.

Boys & Girls Clubs of the Gulf Coast

PASS CHRISTIAN, Mississippi, was ground zero for Hurricane Katrina. When the storm made landfall on August 29, 2005, a tidal surge of ocean water around 30 feet high swept through the town and damaged or destroyed every standing structure. "You could see fields of debris 10 to 15 feet high," recalls David Sykes, executive director of Boys & Girls Clubs of the Gulf Coast. "There were miles and miles of total destruction all along the coastline. It was more than you could comprehend."

Most of the residents of Pass Christian had been evacuated, though many people still had to be rescued. "They were on their roofs, watching cars float by," says Sykes. But the property damage was phenomenal: 86 percent of the town's housing was uninhabitable, and the three schools and the local Boys & Girls Club were reduced to rubble.

Boys & Girls Clubs of America is a nonprofit organization that provides programs and activities for children, families, and communities in need. It operates 4,100 clubs in the United States and US military installations around the world, including six on the Mississippi Gulf Coast, all of which were destroyed by Katrina. With a $5 million grant from the Qatar Katrina Fund, the organization built a new 28,000-square-foot, state-of-the-art club in Pass Christian, right next to the new elementary and middle schools. The club opened in June 2009, replacing a group of trailers that had made do for almost four years. To honor the main donor, the new club was named the Qatar Center.

The soaring steel and glass building includes classrooms, a teen center, a climbing wall, a games room, arts and music centers, a computer technology center, commercial kitchens for learning culinary skills, and a gym that's shared with the school next door. Attendance has doubled in the six years since the club opened, and it hosts around 300 children and teens a day, close to full capacity.

"It has a major impact on the community," says Sydney Wall, president of the club's board. "We do a lot of tutoring after school. It's a safe place for kids who have no one at home." Parents who can afford it pay a small monthly fee; low-income parents (about two-thirds) pay nothing.

"The sheriff in town will also tell you what a positive impact the club has," adds Wall. Sykes agrees: "The stats tell us that the most dangerous time isn't at night; it's from three to eight, after school. That's when crimes are committed by kids, and to kids. A safe club like this reduces that."

Wall says the town had a lot of help right after Katrina. "Because we were the heart of where it hit, people came to us." But the phone call from the Qatar Katrina Fund was still a shock. "Usually people were saying, 'We're going to hold a bake sale,'" she says with a laugh. "But $5 million . . . We are truly, truly grateful."

"I want to help these young people because within this group there are future lawyers and doctors, and we need to help them with their future," noted Qatar's ambassador to the United States at the time, Nasser bin Hamad M. Al-Khalifa. He also praised the project for meeting some of the multiplier goals of the Qatar Katrina Fund: it provided construction jobs in a community hit hard by the hurricane, it would encourage families to stay in the long term, and it was next to a new school, meaning resources could be combined and leveraged for maximum effect. In May 2015, Qatar's present ambassador to the US, Mohammed Jaham Al-Kuwari, visited the center and announced that Qatar had donated a further $30,000.

Like the whole Mississippi Gulf Coast, Pass Christian is still recovering from Hurricane Katrina. The town was also dealt further blows by the 2008 recession and the 2010 Gulf oil spill, which briefly halted the shrimp fishery, one of the few industries still thriving on the coast.

The economy has been battered but is slowly coming back. A small smelter recently opened, and the town's historic church has been rebuilt like new. So have about 40 percent of the houses, to new building codes that lift them high in the air on stilts. And next to the church and the new school sits the Qatar Center, symbol of a town reborn.

The phone call from the Qatar Fund was a surprise to the club. "Usually people were saying, 'We're going to hold a bake sale.' But $5 million? We are truly, truly grateful."

SYDNEY WALL, president of the board, Boys & Girls Clubs of the Gulf Coast

"It's definitely a blessing"

"THIS IS my second home. I can just be myself here," says Dominique Howard. In her second year at Spring Hill College in Mobile, Alabama, 19-year-old Howard is back in Pass Christian, Mississippi, on spring break. Naturally, she has dropped by to visit friends at her second home, the Qatar Centre.

Howard moved to Pass Christian from Las Vegas when she was six years old to live with her grandmother after the death of her parents. She has been going to the Boys & Girls Club ever since. Back then, it was in a refitted building that had once housed the town's African American high school. "My grandmother went there. She was in the last class before they integrated," Howard says. Howard kept going to the club after Katrina, when they had to relocate to trailers. She was in grade eight when they moved to the Qatar Center.

"It's definitely a blessing," Howard says of the new facility. "We're really grateful. It's one of the best centers on the coast. It's really top notch—especially compared to the trailers. It's awesome."

In 2014, Howard was chosen as the Boys & Girls Clubs' Mississippi Youth of the Year. The award was based on her outstanding contributions to her family, school, community, and the club, as well as the personal challenges and obstacles

she overcame. She beat out competitors from the 18 other Mississippi clubs, winning $5,000 in scholarships and going on to the regionals. "I didn't win," she says with a giggle, "but I went to Atlanta, and I got to visit the national headquarters in Nashville. It was awesome!" In 2015, another Qatar Center member, Josh Womble, won the state award and was off to the regionals in July.

"I like it that I don't have to be anyone but myself here," Howard says of the club. "It's helping me become a person I would be proud to know. Every summer I change and grow. The Boys & Girls Clubs influenced who I want to become. I want to be a teacher. I see the importance of that now."

Boys & Girls Clubs of the Gulf Coast

1860

FOUNDED as Boys Club by Mary Goodwin, Alice Goodwin, and Elizabeth Hammersley; renamed Boys & Girls Clubs of America (1990).

4,100

CLUBS across US and at US military installations worldwide.

4 million

YOUTHS SERVED at Qatar Center each year.

18th

MOST PHILANTHROPIC nonprofit organization in US in 2012 (*Chronicle of Philanthropy*).

1,300

YOUTHS SERVED at Qatar Center each day.

$5 million

FUND NAME: Boys & Girls Clubs of the Gulf Coast

OBJECTIVE: Rebuild Boys & Girls Clubs community center destroyed by Katrina.

RESULTS: Built 28,000-square-foot, state-of-the-art Qatar Center next to new elementary and middle schools.

66%

CLUB YOUTHS are economically disadvantaged.

51%

CLUB YOUTHS live in single-parent households.

About Qatar

THE STATE OF QATAR occupies a small peninsula roughly the size of Connecticut on the western edge of the Arabian Gulf. The country is encircled by 300 miles of sparkling coastline, except for a short 37-mile border with Saudi Arabia, and over 90 percent of it is desert. The Gulf's famously salty water produces particularly luminous pearls, and for many centuries Qatar's economy was led by pearling, which made the country a thriving center of trade in the region. Today, pearl diving is a celebration of traditional culture.

Working with many American companies and other partners, Qatar has developed its abundant oil and natural gas resources to become a major global energy exporter. Supported by one of the largest proven natural gas reserves in the world, Qatar is the world's richest nation per capita, with an estimated GDP of $323.3 billion.

Most residents live in the capital, Doha, known for its ultramodern skyline, scenic waterfront promenade, numerous museums and historic sites, and the *Souq Waqif*, an outdoor market. Doha boasts a lively culture, hosting annual music, food, and other cultural festivals; motor shows; and sports tournaments. Its sights include the Museum of Islamic Art, an iconic building designed by I. M. Pei, and Katara Cultural Village, which includes theaters, concert halls, galleries, and restaurants, and hosts artistic events and organizations such as the Doha Film Institute.

< **THE SKYLINE OF DOHA**, capital of Qatar

From 1995, Qatar emerged as a model for peace and moderate liberalization in the Gulf region under the leadership of the Father Amir, His Highness Sheikh Hamad bin Khalifa Al-Thani. Advanced health care, education, a free press, and voting rights for women were established. In June 2013, His Highness Sheikh Tamim bin Hamad Al-Thani succeeded his father as Amir, continuing with the long-term plan to stimulate the country's economic, social, human, and environmental development.

This plan, Qatar National Vision 2030, stresses a competitive and diversified economy beyond relying on hydrocarbon resources. Qatar's expanded global economic reach is evident in increased investments in the United States, which have created thousands of jobs across America. These include partnerships with numerous American companies, such as Exxon Mobil, ConocoPhillips, and Raytheon, and real estate investments, such as the revitalization project CityCenterDC (in Washington, DC).

The relationship between the two countries is reciprocal: Qatar is home to many Americans, and the United States is both Qatar's largest foreign investor and its largest source of imports. Qatar is also a close ally of the United States and an advocate of building a peaceful and prosperous Middle East. In 1992, the two countries signed a comprehensive defense

cooperation agreement, and Qatar is host to the Al Udeid Air Base, a key operational center for US forces in the region.

Qatar places great emphasis on education. Doha's expansive Education City is home to branch campuses of six prestigious US universities: Carnegie Mellon, Georgetown, Northwestern, Texas A&M, Virginia Commonwealth, and Weill Cornell. All of these offer degree programs identical to those on their US campuses, and attract students from across the Middle East and around the world. Their presence has brought a culturally rich and diverse expatriate community to Qatar and has augmented ties to the United States. The Qatar Foundation, which created Education City, hopes to see the country transition to a knowledge-based economy in the coming decades.

Qatar is also home to Al Jazeera, a global media network that reaches an estimated 270 million households around the world. Founded in 1996, Al Jazeera now has 82 bureaus worldwide and broadcasts in three continents, second only to the BBC in reach. By broadcasting dissenting views and encouraging debate, Al Jazeera has transformed the media landscape. Plans are underway to launch a second satellite in 2016.

In 2022, Qatar will become the first Arab country to host the FIFA World Cup, the globe's biggest sports tournament. Spurred by the upcoming event, new infrastructure projects are unfolding in Doha, including a metro system, a light-rail system, roads, stadiums, and other sporting infrastructure.

∧ **THE MUSEUM OF ISLAMIC ART** in Doha includes manuscripts, textiles, ceramics, and other works spanning 1,400 years

The State of Qatar

2,123,160

ESTIMATED POPULATION.

$323.3 billion

ESTIMATED GDP, making it the richest country per capita today.

13%

OF WORLD'S LNG reserves (25 trillion cubic meters); 3rd-largest reserve in the world.

92%

OF EXPORT EARNINGS from oil and gas.

$121.2 billion

EXPORTS; $39.12 billion imports; US is largest foreign investor and largest source of imports (14.2%).

120

U.S. COMPANIES operate in Qatar.

$11 billion

DEFENSE AGREEMENT signed between Qatar and US.

2022

FIFA WORLD CUP will be held in Qatar, first Arab country to host world's most watched sporting event.

2009

QATAR'S Department of International Development established under Ministry of Foreign Affairs.

2012

HUMANITARIAN partnership agreement signed with UN to coordinate Qatar's global humanitarian responses.

26th-largest

GOVERNMENT PROVIDER of humanitarian assistance in last decade.

$2.5 billion

ESTIMATED government humanitarian aid distributed 2010–2015, making foreign aid and development integral part of foreign policy.

$5.4 billion

COMMITTED to rebuild Gaza, along with US and other countries.

$20 million

GIVEN in 2010 to Qatar Haiti Fund; $100 million given in 2011 to Japanese earthquake and tsunami relief; $3.3 million being raised for 2015 Nepal earthquake relief, as well as 180 tons of relief material and a field hospital.

Qatar Foreign Aid

THE GOVERNMENT of Qatar sees humanitarian aid as a key element of its foreign policy and culture. The state is among the most active in the international community in development and humanitarian aid, providing millions of dollars to almost 100 countries each year. Between 2006 and 2013, Qatar's foreign aid allocations were among the highest in the world relative to GDP.

The Qatari foreign aid strategy aims to achieve sustainable change in war-stricken or impoverished regions, or in areas recovering from environmental disaster. In this last decade, relief and reconstruction funding have focused on disaster areas such as the US Gulf Coast (Hurricane Katrina, 2005), Port-au-Prince (Haiti earthquake, 2010), Tōhoku (Japan earthquake, 2011), and Nepal (earthquakes, 2015). In 2013 alone, Qatari foreign aid reached nearly $1.8 billion.

Qatar Haiti Fund

AT THE 2010 UN International Donors' Conference, Towards a New Future for Haiti, Qatar pledged $20 million to Haiti's reconstruction in the wake of the devastating earthquake that year. Qatar has since disbursed more than $6 million to various ongoing renewal programs. Focusing on infrastructure development projects, youth empowerment, and education, the Qatar Haiti Fund (QHF) has helped to restore communities and safeguard the country from future natural disasters.

IN 2012, the QHF committed $2 million to Partners in Health to create mobile health-care clinics to deliver primary care services and vaccines to the most remote areas of Haiti. Hôpital Albert Schweitzer, in central Haiti, received $87,000 to fund training programs, buy supplies, and create internal protocols. A further $75,000 was disbursed to a nonprofit organization dedicated to building sustainable communities by training people in hygiene standards, shelter construction, and HIV/AIDS prevention.

In partnership with the United States Agency for International Development (USAID), the QHF has provided $5 million to build "Qatar City," a community of 148 homes, a vocational school, and a commercial area in the city of Cabaret. The area is being developed as a state-of-the-art, environmentally integrated, disaster-resistant community by the United Nations Office for Project Services (UNOPS). The expected completion date is in 2016.

The QHF has also pledged $5.5 million in partnership with the Clinton Foundation to rebuild the Faculté des Sciences at the Université d'Etat d'Haïti, one of the oldest and most prestigious universities in Port-au-Prince, Haiti's capital. This project aims to establish an educational hub in the recovering city.

Qatar Friendship Fund

THE QATAR FRIENDSHIP FUND (QFF) allocated $100 million to the rehabilitation of child education centers, health programs, and fishery infrastructure in several areas in Tōhoku, Japan, affected by the catastrophic earthquake, tsunami, and nuclear disaster of 2011.

The first reconstruction project, a $23 million fish processing plant, opened in October 2012, in Onagawa (Miyagi Prefecture). The plant helped rebuild devastated local fishing economies, the backbone of the region's economy before the disaster. The QFF created thousands of job opportunities for fishing communities and helped to reduce environmental damage and contamination to marine life.

The QFF also funded approximately $24 million of educational development projects, mostly focused on child education and children with disabilities. The expansion of schools and learning and recreation centers provided relief for tens of thousands of children and families suffering from the effects of the nuclear disaster.

Other projects are underway. In November 2014, for instance, the Qatar Sports Park opened in Shirakawa, a city that had to be evacuated following the Fukushima nuclear disaster in 2011. The facility will help to reinvigorate the lives the 150,000 people in Shirakawa and environs.

Special thanks to our generous sponsors

ConocoPhillips congratulates the State of Qatar on the creation of the Qatar Katrina Fund. The impact made by the fund over the last decade brought relief, rebuilding, and renewed hope to all those affected by the devastating storm. On behalf of ConocoPhillips employees worldwide, we're proud to support and join the celebration marking the 10th anniversary of the fund. We are uplifted by the joyful messages of triumph and resilience captured in this commemorative book. The generosity extended by the people of Qatar demonstrates that the best way to overcome hardship and despair is friends reaching out to help friends.

Raytheon

Thanks to those who helped make this book possible

The Times-Picayune

page two :

Everyone who contributed
And to all of you who shared your experiences

Embassy of the State of Qatar
2555 M Street NW, Washington DC USA 20037
www.qatarembassy.net

Printed and bound in Canada by Friesens

15 16 17 18 19 5 4 3 2 1

Produced by PAGE TWO STRATEGIES
Text by SCOTT STEEDMAN
Principal photography by RUSH JAGOE
Design and art direction by PETER COCKING

Additional text: foreword (pp. 14–15) by Mitch Landrieu; introduction (pp. 16–17) by His Excellency Mohammed Jaham Al-Kuwari; profile of Etta May Williams (p. 57) adapted from 2008 annual report of Qatar Katrina Fund; profiles of Arthur Anderson, Barbara Lopez, Shawanda Leggins, and Frank Myers and Lasonja Washington (pp. 63–67) adapted from testimonials provided by Neighborhood Housing Services, with additional reporting by Scott Steedman; March of Dimes/ Gretchen Deeves text (pp. 109–10) adapted from 2008 annual report of Qatar Katrina Fund.

Additional photography: Cheryl Gerber (pp. 8, 34, 54, 70, 76, 82, 102, 103, 110, 118–120, 137, 152); Chip Somodevilla/Getty Images (p. 12); the *Times-Picayune*/NOLA.com (pp. 18, 23 top right); Dan Anderson/eps/Corbis (p. 21); Habitat for Humanity International (pp. 23 top left; 24); Shutterstock/ Imagist (p. 23 bottom right); iStock/Mario Tama/ EdStock (p. 23 bottom left); Memorial Hospital at Gulfport (pp. 25, 90, 93, 99); Richard Tucker/ Xavier University (p. 135); courtesy Sean O'Keefe (p. 181); iStock/Mlenny (p. 200); iStock/Frank Vanden Berg (p. 202 top); iStock/Sean Gallup/ EdStock (p. 202 bottom); courtesy Qatar Embassy (p. 203); Céline Lefebvre (p. 204); iStock/Claudiad (p. 207 left); Shutterstock/AVAVA (p. 207 right).